FOR THE TIME BEING

VERCORS

For the Time Being

Translated by
JONATHAN GRIFFIN

HUTCHINSON OF LONDON

HUTCHINSON & CO. (*Publishers*) LTD
178–202 Great Portland Street, London, W.1

London Melbourne Sydney
Auckland Bombay Toronto
Johannesburg New York

First published in France
under the title Pour Prendre Congé.
Published in Great Britain 1960

This book has been set in Baskerville type
face. It has been printed in Great Britain on
Antique Wove paper by Taylor Garnett
Evans & Co. Ltd., Watford, Herts, and
bound by them

This book appeared in France in December 1957, several months before the events of 13 May, which the author forecast, and General de Gaulle's accession to power.

It should have appeared in Great Britain soon afterwards. But various circumstances, among them the printing strike, postponed its publication. In spite of the interval it has lost none of its topicality. The author still stands by his decision and is keeping apart from all public activity, his view being that for him this could only end on the barricades or in prison.

CONTENTS

Speech on the Moscow Radio

Final Intervention

I die of thirst although the fountain's near

OR THE BROKEN VESSEL

THIS is not a book, it is a file.

Of documents in the story of one of those characters in the comedy of modern politics who are known as *potiches d'honneur* – 'big pots' that adorn platforms and ceremonies.

I have been playing this unrewarding part for over twelve years. I do not complain. I might, if I had wished, have played a more active part, supposing I had had the time or the temperament. I had not, and so I served in my station, where I could. I have no regrets: I was useful in my fashion, and that is all that matters.

But the day comes when the vessel is all chipped and cracked and is no longer presentable – when it becomes absurd for it to appear on the display shelf.

It will still be useful, but in a less proud part. It will not now be used to put flowers in, but to store grain or flour. Some people may be sorry, what of that? Let them blame the breakers.

For it seems to be true that *potiches d'honneur* obey the same law as all china: they are more often broken than worn out. It is too late to mend them, they will not hold water. I agree that it is a pity: if you have been made into a *potiche d'honneur*, this probably means that you did enjoy a certain authority in the minds of part of the public. And so every vessel, when new, represents a measurable social value. Its diminution under the blows of the clumsy – or worse – may be all sorts of things but not an increase of wealth. Besides, for the vase the misfortune is usually a double one, for it is blamed for the deterioration it has undergone as though it were the cause of it; its presence shocks people, they blame it for that, and so it becomes slightly less presentable still. This is sad for it, but what is to be done? Except reluctantly to admit the facts as they are, and to take the consequences.

And yet the process which leads to such a result – how a vase gets knocked about until it becomes useless – is perhaps not altogether without interest. That is why I am publishing this *dossier*. This is not the first time I have given readers the documents of a case. I did so, some time ago, for the dispute over the Rajk affair, in which I was opposed to my Communist friends. Then also, as objectively as I could, I left it to the reader to judge and to find me right or wrong. For I admit frankly that I am incapable of judging my own acts myself. Like everyone else, I am subject to my moods, to my *amour propre*, to the whole mechanism of self-defence which conceals from the party to a case his own faults and his own mistakes. And indeed what is interesting, it seems to me, is not whether people agree with me or not, or whether they applaud my discernment or laugh at my naïveté: this would not have the slightest importance for world history. The interest of such a publication lies, I think, partly in the facts themselves, and partly in the conflicts which these have aroused between persons or groups who were in agreement about almost everything else and who, but for them, would probably have remained so.

Now once more – no doubt for the last time – I am submitting the documents objectively, just as they are, to those who may take an interest in this sort of thing. Those who already feel they cannot give the author the minimum of credit – of confidence, of friendly interest, or at least curiosity – will have no need of a warning not to read further; they will already have understood that they will be bored stiff.

For this is really a file, a *dossier*, and nothing else. A disordered *dossier* consisting of a series of essays, articles, declarations, open letters, private letters and so forth, none of which I have been willing to omit,[1] not even when they are what I no

---

[1] Translator's note: In this English edition there are certain cuts, sanctioned by the author.

longer would write, or would now write differently. There are,
therefore, to be found among them all sorts of contradictions,
of feelings or opinions that are apparently irreconcilable. I have
decided not to bring them in line by retouching them, and this
means that anyone who wishes will be able to lay hold of them
in order to beat me with rods which I myself will have placed
in his hands: my friends because I part company with them for
a time, their opponents because I obstinately refuse to join them.
The former will find in my past writings plenty of ammunition
for condemning my present withdrawal, and the latter will find
a fine harvest of inconsistencies with which to accuse me once
again of duplicity. What if they do? The vase will simply be
a little less usable. A little more or a little less, in the state it's
in. . . .

   'The dying man has licence to say all,'

writes Villon in his *Testament*, and the same applies to a political
potiche when it has served its time. The final service it can
honestly do is the ultimate sincerity of 'saying all' in order that
its successors may draw the lesson. Hence my decision to publish
these pages just as they are and to abstain from those cleverly
concealed evasions or flattering slants which consist in a tiny
alteration here, a slight cut there and a modest addition a little
farther on. Where I have introduced occasional comments,
I have done so merely to fill in the chronological gaps and
provide the indispensable bridges. I have tried to be personally
as detached as is humanly possible – not to 'plead' and not
even to explain, simply to inform. I hope I have succeeded.

              .   .   .   .   .

A *dossier*, then – or a testament. Because in fact I am publishing these pages as a result of the decision I have taken to
withdraw for a time from public life and its struggles.
   I have no illusions: public life will not let me be, even though
I doff my hat to it. Doffing one's hat to it is not so easy. 'Poor
Villon' would have liked to, no doubt. Society and I (it can't be
helped) are two. And the powers that be: that makes three.

I cannot hope they will suddenly behave in such a way that I shall be able calmly to remain silent, or to hum *amen*. I am not condemning myself to perpetual silence. All I mean is that I have decided – for the present – not to speak at meetings or rallies, not to appear on the platforms of congresses, and not to add my name at the bottom of lists of signatures. In short, I have decided to leave the stage.

'Very nice too! Do, if you like: but don't make a fuss about it!' I am not making a fuss, but here is my problem: that I cannot consent, either, to retire without a word, on tiptoe. The reasons for retiring are too serious for that. At the same time I am still less willing to do as others have done and resign with *éclat* from this body or that. I am obliged, therefore, to give some explanation.

I shall not walk out of anything – not from the C.N.E.[1] or the Peace Movement or the Resistance Associations or from any of the bodies of which I am president, vice-president, honorary president, honorary member, or anything of the sort. I do not wish to harm anything or anyone, and above all I do not wish any such resignation to be open to exploitation by the opponents whom we still have in common.

I do not wish to leave these organizations: I wish to keep aloof from them for a time. In my 'Portrait' of General Brosset I told of the letter I received from him after the collapse of France. It was sent from the Panama Canal and bore this arresting date: 10 May 1940. He had not yet heard the news of the launching of the German invasion and this is what he wrote to me: 'All that I know about the war that is preparing, all that the war in Poland has taught us, I have verified day by day from my observation post. All through the winter I never ceased sounding the alarm. But the innumerable attacks and obstacles and instances of obstinacy on this side and on that, made the position untenable. So I have been kicked upstairs, and am about to teach the Columbians what the French Army is unwilling to learn.

'After all, it is better so. When I get back, if, as I hope, the enemy is still hesitating, perhaps France will at last have

[1] Comité National des Ecrivains.

emerged from this fatal sleep and I shall kiss the Awakened
Beauty. Let us hope so! If not, if the enemy does not wait, it will
be better to have had no truck with what will happen then.'

That is exactly what I think today, and what has made me
decide on withdrawal. If Fascism in France does not wait;
if the French people, if the working class under the leadership
of its own party, continue to play at being Sleeping Beauties
– the left-wingers to fight among themselves and exclude one
another, and the smashers of vases to destroy each other's; if the
Republicans in the Assembly continue, out of incredible blindness or incredible flabbiness, to vote for the forgers of the chains
that are being prepared for the Republic – I in my turn think
that it will be better to have had no truck with the things that
will happen then.

The pages of this book too are made up of 'innumerable
attacks and obstacles and instances of obstinacy on this side and
on that' which, as in the other case, have made the position
untenable. I have not been kicked upstairs and exiled to Columbia, but exile for me is here –

'In my own land I am a foreigner' –

since I have everywhere had my mouth shut and been contained
within a silence so complete that, really, Columbia sometimes
seems to me less distant than the Paris Press or Radio-Télévision
Française.

.   .   .   .   .

Not that this is the first time I have felt the temptation to
bow my way out. Only this time I am doing it.

It is, as I write, exactly thirteen years ago that I first
announced my intention of leaving the scene – before I had
even come on it. Six or eight of us had met as we did every
Wednesday in a clandestine refuge of the *Editions de Minuit*, and
we could almost hear the rumble of the approaching tanks of
Patton's army. The committee was facing the question of the
future of the publishing firm, once Paris was liberated. I
said:

'Do you think it would be wise for us to show ourselves in the open immediately?'

All speaking at once, they asked me what I meant.

'If we reveal ourselves,' I said, 'our boats are burned. But if we stay clandestine, we remain available in case of need.'

A fine rumpus followed: 'Available for what?' 'What need?' 'Are you mad?'

'Are you so certain,' I persisted, 'that America will be so favourable to us? That she won't prefer to negotiate with Pétain or Laval, rather than with the Resistance and the Communists?'

The fear was an exaggerated one, I agree. Or let us say, premature. Fundamentally, I was not wildly wrong. A little previous perhaps. I have never ceased to descry, beneath the sleeping eyelids of Fascism, the steely gleam of an eye watching for its revenge. To be sure, I never imagined at that time what our present resistant ministers would turn into. Neither did they, no doubt. Reality nearly always excels the wildest imagination. Anyhow, nobody on that day was willing to share my fears.

'Well,' I added, 'you can do what you like; but as for me – Vercors – you must promise me secrecy: I shall stay anonymous.'

'But that's impossible!' they cried.

And they explained to me why, as to a child: my *nom de guerre*, whether I liked it or not, had acquired the colours of an emblem, which would be needed daily during the great renewal. The new Press, at last independent and clean, would have need of it; so would the Resistance Associations, those moral guarantors of the parties and of their single and indivisible brotherhood; so would that of the writers, to separate neatly the grain from the chaff; so would our cultural links with the Allies, united for ever to guarantee peace; etc. etc. Vercors, they said, cannot vanish. And so I watched the merciless and cumbersome vase with which I was to be loaded being manufactured before my alarmed eyes.

I fought tooth and nail. I said they had got the wrong man. I was a lone wolf, an incorrigible country bumpkin, incapable of saying two words in public without writing them down first, incapable of writing them without feeling a violent need to do so; an accidental writer enjoying an accidental fame, which would soon be exploded by M. Paulhan and his friends in the coming literary battles. How long would I really be of any use? Three months, perhaps six – after which I would be forgotten, thrown away like old rubbish, and the unfortunate Bruller with me. No, thank you!

Had not a grand old man covered with honours said to me – this, it is true, was a little later – 'Ah, Vercors, how you interest me! Like you, glory fell on me all of a sudden, when I was more or less your age, because of a war book. Just take advantage of it! It will never be as pure as it is today. Later on, you will have to fight to keep it!' As I had not the slightest intention of fighting, I was warned of what was in store for me. I had seen so many examples already! I remembered a prophetic drawing by Bofa in his *Synthèses Littéraires*: an enormous wooden cross[1] dragged along by the writer whom it had made famous and crushing him. I could foresee the cartoon someone would draw of me, with my book like a millstone round my neck, drowning in the silence of the sea. . . . Above all, I remembered that unfortunate hero of the First World War, ephemerally famous for having, under a hellish bombardment, shouted out a memorable war-cry: many years later, having no other title to put after his name, being neither an academician nor a minister, he still sometimes appeared on the posters announcing some important ceremony, with the following absurd and touching description:

Jacques PERICARD
who raised the sublime battle cry: 'Up the dead!'

Was I going to allow people to turn me into someone whom, one day, the printed programmes would recall to the forgetful under the nickname 'Vercors-who-wrote-the-sublime-book-*The-Silence-of-the-Sea*'? No, thanks very much, gentlemen!

The fear was an exaggerated one, I agree. Or let us say

---

[1] The allusion is to *Les Croix de Bois*, the book through which Roland Dorgelès became well known.

premature. Fundamentally, I was not wildly wrong. Perhaps a little previous. Under the amiable scraping bows of so many people who came up to me, all the more anxious to bow to me the less anxious they had been to take part in the Resistance, I could always see the future eagerness to kick back. Certainly I never imagined at that time that some writers of the Resistance would one day excel them in malice towards me. Nor could they, no doubt. However that may be, I was beaten, and I understood with dread and irony that I was one of those men who rarely yield to their own weaknesses but yield to any appeal made to their feeling of duty. That, too, is a weakness, and one of the worst: for one is yielding merely to other people's reason instead of sticking firmly to one's own. That is nothing to be proud of.

And so I became a *potiche d'honneur*, and what I had foreseen was not long in happening – as well as many other things which I had not foreseen.

· · · · ·

I had certainly foreseen that the unfortunate Bruller, whose one delight was to draw and engrave, to live in the country, to wander about dreamily, to build boats and sail them on the sea and to enjoy the simple life with a few friends chosen for their loyalty, would more or less disappear within the shadow of a writer who had become too abruptly famous and was now to be cooked and eaten with all the sauces of public life. I did not foresee that he and his work would disappear so completely and that ten years later he would hardly survive in my own memory except as a far off and nostalgic shade. I had certainly foreseen that the unfortunate Bruller, who in twenty years – a rather rare occurrence which perhaps tells in his favour – had not lost a single one of his friends and had not even experienced the shadow of a quarrel between them and him, would not keep them all: I had certainly foreseen that Vercors, the usurper, no longer the sole master of his actions and words (and in addition – the unfairness of it! – too suddenly famous for too slender a work), would lose some of them. I did not foresee that I should lose so many and so quickly. Or that the first and most disappointing of these betrayals would come immediately, just after the Liberation. That a man whom, during fifteen years of warm friendship, I had respected above the rest would pursue me with calumnies for refusing to travesty in an epic (featuring his latest mistress) the story of a shared adventure, too simple for such treatment. Even today, it seems, he has not laid down his arms. . . . This constancy bewilders me. I had certainly foreseen that the *Editions de Minuit* and their director would be fought by the other publishing houses, the more bitterly the less clear were their consciences about the past. I did not foresee that I should soon myself be kicked out, together with the spirit that had reigned there, while a Trojan horse introduced by me would open the gates to recantation – that is to say, to the diametrically opposed influence of our main rival.

The lesson was clear: I was too disarmed, and that jungle was no place for me. Had I not known this from the first day? It would have been a lesson worth learning, no doubt, at least if I could have acted on it. But I was immediately called upon to go and tell the Germans what the Resistance had meant; to go and take part in the founding of the Peace Movement in Poland. And the *potiche d'honneur*, in spite of the strong temptation it then felt to return to the peace of the countryside, remained faithful to its post. By doing so, it attached itself with fresh bonds to its shelf. And besides, my situation was changing. After the flow, the ebb. As the prestige of the Resistance – the respect it aroused or the fear it inspired – declined, and with that prestige the halo that had crowned those who had served it; and as the author-of-*The-Silence-of-the-Sea* became more and more like (as he had foreseen) the lieutenant-who-raised-the-sublime-battle-cry; as he descended the steps of his accidental celebrity to reach once more the less brilliant but more authentic – and therefore more questionable – level of his true worth: not only did he cease to lose friends and affections, but he began to win new ones – disinterested ones – and to win back old ones – intimidated for a time – and with them the simple taste for living which so many mortifications had weakened. And I recovered at the same time a part of my former life, its rustic

B

calm, security and simple pleasures. I have enemies, as everyone has, but out in the open. The people who give me a smile are no longer concealing a knuckle-duster behind their backs, and I can return their smiles with confidence.

And yet it is now that I have once more decided to doff my hat and go, and this time I am doing it.

.   .   .   .   .

If, just now, I allowed myself to show a glimpse of one or two old personal ordeals (and I have not mentioned the cruellest of them), this was not done for the pleasure of 'unpacking my heart with words': it was to show that these trials had not sufficed to produce this decision and, therefore, that the taking of the decision precisely when these trials are fading into the past means that the new reasons for it must be pretty strong.

Not strong enough (I repeat this to avoid any ambiguity) to make me withdraw into my shell, protected from blows. I fear there will be plenty of those soon enough, and although I am the opposite of a pugnacious man I have never been able to keep outside the *mêlée*. I doubt if I ever shall. I am not 'decommitting' myself. It is most unlikely that I shall be found absent from the coming barricades against a Fascism which is every day gaining ground.

But I shall not fight – *for the time being* – in the ranks of organized bodies. And yet I have always thought, and still think, that the isolated combatant is not very effective. In spite of this, I must make up my mind, for the moment, to a solitary struggle. (I would give a great deal to be mistaken.) But what I could bear still less would be to dissimulate in order to keep the warmth of companionship – the reassurance and sense of brotherhood which this companionship gives. Unfortunately, in the various positions I have taken up in the face of the events that have occurred since the Twentieth Congress of the Communist Party in the U.S.S.R., there is no group – and practically no individual – that has not, in one way or another, more or less condemned me: even when they have not more or less openly made it clear to me that, in the interests of the very causes which I defend, I was becoming undesirable or embarrassing. To doff my hat and go is the logical and inevitable conclusion from this situation and from my isolation – I regret it with all my heart – imposed upon me by this silent, often friendly, but almost unanimous disavowal. Of the authority once enjoyed (though every day slightly less) by the bright *potiche d'honneur* of the Liberation, there remains no more than a washed-out memory, along with the now scarcely decorative form of that cracked crock which-wrote-the-sublime-book. I loathe playing this part. It has become as unpleasing to others as it is to myself. And it is no longer any use to anybody. Or else it is of use for deception.

This book is my last act as *potiche d'honneur*. A testament, in fact. I hope it will not one day be seen as having constituted, for many of us, a *de profundis*. The time for hanging on is past – for me. This is not the first time I have decided to doff my hat and go.

But this time I mean it.

The Goodnight Ballade

This fifty-fifth year of my age
I've drunk the dregs of defamation,
not all a fool, not all a sage
for all the knocks of my vocation,
which filled me up to saturation
like a good mug of Isigny. . . .
Big pot I was, with pride of station.
Who can deny what all could see?

But if I took as in my favour
those smilings fair and speeches fine
of highly disappointing savour,
look now at this my sad decline:
a poor old pot, condemned to pine
high on its shelf in lonely fate,
unsteady, cracked with line on line.
Let none think I exaggerate.

And now, if any reprimands me
and says that he's by me maligned,
not so! If he but understands me
he'll see I have no axe to grind.
Here's all the malice of my mind:
If to me mercy at heart he bore,
he shall go straight to Paradise
with or without his poor Vercors.

. . . .

Princes, the time to pipe and caper
is past. Sit down, Bruller, and listen
(have you your pen and ink and paper?).
Here beginneth the first lesson.

Bare as a Worm, Clad like a President

M Y polemics with my fellow-writers of the French Communist Party have been going on for ten years.
They began on the ground of principles, and it was
indeed for the choice of this ground that I was reproached. 'Is
there such a thing as morality in politics?' I asked – and my
answer was in the affirmative; but I was met with the objection
that such a question, if raised like that in the abstract, was
meaningless. Pierre Hervé accused me with some violence, in
the name of realism, of playing into the hands of the Machiavellis of *bourgeois* morality (a few years later he was to reproach
me, in the name of morality, of playing into the hands of the
Machiavellis of realism). Victor Leduc rejected what he called
'the Jesuitical dilemma of end and means', and refused to draw
up 'an abstract catalogue of forbidden or legitimate means',
adding that, for anyone who takes as his aim the liberation of
man, anything that debases man is obviously ruled out. To my
question: 'But precisely, which are these things that debase
man?' I could get no answer – because obviously such an
answer would have constituted 'an abstract catalogue'. . . . I
mentioned, as an instance, anti-Semitism: did he mean that, in
certain circumstances, they were reserving the right to use this
as a political force? The rejoinder came: 'The question is a
provocative one, since race discrimination is obviously irreconcilable with Marxism.' I expected that statement, though I did
not fail to point out that it was completely abstract. They had
had, in the end, to meet me on my own ground.
A highly concrete problem was, alas, soon to arise: that of

the Rajk affair. In an article published in *Esprit* I denounced
the lie which the whole of that trial was, from the judges to
the prisoner. I was then reproached for having played into the
hands of the enemies of the working class by accusing the
Communists of lying. 'But it is *to* the Communists that the lies
are being told!' I protested. 'If you are sure I am wrong, let us
discuss it openly before them.' I was not allowed this; and from
that day I ceased to write for the Communist Press and in
particular for the *Lettres Françaises*, because I could no longer
express myself freely there.

Later there came the Slansky affair and that of the 'white-
coated assassins'. We fell head over heels into the very thing
I had chosen as an example – anti-Semitism: was there or was
there not, in the U.S.S.R. and elsewhere, an anti-Semitic
policy? The position of the Communists was then reversed:
because anti-Semitism obviously has its place in the catalogue of
forbidden means, *therefore* (they said to me in substance) there
cannot be anti-Semitism under a Socialist régime. Q.E.D.

Thus they refused to examine the concrete reality, in the
name of the catalogued and abstract morality which they had
so firmly refused to recognize not long before. I was unable to
discuss this disquieting reversal publicly, because the violence
of the attacks by our common adversaries had put me in a
position where I must either remain silent or find myself in their
camp.[1] A few weeks later the release of the doctors settled the
question for the moment and appeared to prove the Communists right. I was delighted. But it left the fundamental
problem unsolved: were our adversaries right or not, and was
the ethic of Communism, or was it not, double-faced – one day
condemning unreservedly all abstract morality, and the next
day having recourse to it, according to the convenience of the
moment, without batting an eyelid? If it was, the relations of
a man like myself with the Communist writers became
difficult. . . .

A few months later, in the Eastern republics, there began
the first rumours, the confessions of error and the rehabilita-
tions. Then there burst the thunderclap of the Twentieth

[1] Cf. *Les Pas dans le Sable* (pp. 197–236).

Congress, which showed our fears to have been so terribly well founded, and not only, alas, justified them all but revealed that they were far exceeded in number and gravity by the reality.

This confronted me with an imperative dilemma, which it was impossible to evade: for seven years I had agreed to keep my lips sealed, because, though I no longer wanted to write in the Communist Press, I refused to become an auxiliary of the enemies of Communism in the *bourgeois* Press. Would the columns that had been closed to me be now, in the light of this disastrous experience, open to me, and would I in future be allowed to make known in them my points of disagreement or uneasiness, in order that fresh errors – fresh crimes – might be opposed before, rather than after, they had produced their pernicious consequences? If the answer was 'No' and if I was expected to continue to keep my lips sealed, I should no longer have the excuse of uncertainty, or even the cowardly but convenient excuse of naïveté: this time I should be knowingly making myself into an accomplice of future errors or crimes. I realized that I would have to fight. I fought. It went on for a year. I hoped to be supported in this fight by those of my colleagues whom the revelations of the Twentieth Congress had confronted with the same dilemma. I was, quite often, verbally, in private. Unfortunately, I was not in public and by deeds. And it was amid almost general consent that I listened to the following reply, after all my efforts: 'It is our turn to speak, and yours to keep quiet.' I do not reproach the Communists, who had reduced me to silence when Rajk was being executed, for wishing to draw the moral of the story themselves, and to dress up in their turn, even though rather late in the day, as redressers of wrongs done: better late than never. But since they are refusing me the right to exercise with them my freedom of expression, refusing it categorically, for tomorrow as for today; and since I cannot bring myself, either, to write in the papers which attack them; and since I am also unwilling to keep my lips sealed in future in what would be mute complicity: only one attitude is left open to me – to withdraw into silence, but at the top of my voice. This then is what I am doing by publishing the pages that follow in this chapter, none of which was allowed to see the light. They depict clearly the disappointing struggle I have carried on for over a year behind closed doors – until I lost.

.   .   .   .   .

Just after the Twentieth Congress, at a time when I was in Italy, I received from one of my Communist friends who at the moment of the Rajk affair had shown me by inexorable logic how wrong I was, a letter about a preface, with a postscript containing this admission: 'I have just re-read your article in Esprit. *You were right, Vercors, as I was wrong. But in still keeping confidence in us, you have been right against Them.' This* bona fide *avowal had its value, provided the author and his friends went on honestly to act on it. I therefore answered at once, to mark the event and to reserve my judgement.*

Florence 17 April 1956.

Thank you for the preface. You will certainly be surprised to learn that I share your opinion on all the nice things it says about me personally, and do not share it on the things it says against my thesis. That is, no doubt, part of my infernal obstinacy. I continue stubbornly to think that, precisely when all men are living in the Golden Age of material facilities and in the midst of universal liberty available *ad infinitum*, the chief, if not the only, problem that will remain to be solved by them will be to face up finally to the question of life's purpose. And if they hit on the wrong answer, what a mess! . . .

Talking of a mess, your postscript about Rajk leaves me rather perplexed. I have been away from Paris for a month and have to rely on the papers (the Italian ones at that): I know nothing about what is really happening in France. And in particular I don't know what you are really thinking.

I mean – seriously – that to have been right when you were wrong in '49 has not the slightest importance to me. But that you should have been wrong is much more important, it seems to me, for you and me and everyone. For to have been wrong in these circumstances has very grave implications. The execution of an innocent man is as criminal in Hungary as in America.

The mystery of the confessions is no less frightening. The deepest disagreement at that time was not so much about which of us was seeing clearly, you or me, but about whether or not it was right to inform the opinion of the Communist masses of so disquieting a doubt. The answer given to me was that it was not. And so they were misled, with the involuntary complicity of those who gave me that 'No'. What conclusions do the Communists draw today from these events? If all there is to be is a distribution of awards – 'You were right and we were wrong, and that is that' – this would be no less grave now than it was when the crime was committed in the midst of that silence which I was prevented from breaking. This is why – apart from the fact that I would like to know your own opinion – I am wondering, with a certain uneasiness, whether the Communist Press will allow me today what it forbade me yesterday? Whether I may draw for Communist readers the lesson of this whole business? In other words, whether I am to be granted now the confidence I was refused then; whether the trust I have put in the Party through all these years, in spite of this fundamental disagreement, might this time be repaid?

This is no rhetorical curiosity. I shall have to draw the lesson one way or another. I cannot evade the more or less indignant letters I receive from anguished readers, who remind me of that old dispute and ask me, in substance: 'And now what?' The question is the same as before: where am I to answer? in what columns? What I am allowed or refused will have great significance.

I received no answer: and when, a fortnight later, during the Annual General Meeting of the Comité National des Ecrivains, of which I was president, I made the speech which follows, I had no idea how it would be received, having only returned to France a few days before:

Since the wind that is blowing at present is apparently a breeze of self-criticism, I propose this evening to conduct my own and ours.

When I say ours, I do not mean exactly that of the C.N.E. as an association. Our secretary-general will tell you shortly that this year has been uneventful for our association. And that is true. But perhaps it was not so for all our members.

The revelations of the Twentieth Congress at Moscow have, in fact, repercussions beyond the strictly political field. Innocent people have been put to death, and this involves, within everyone's conscience and particularly in that of writers, their most private feeling for morality and justice and, in general, their whole idea of the relations between thought and action. We have all of us, Communist or not, to examine ourselves honestly in this new light, we must all of us ask ourselves whether what we have done during these recent years was really what we wanted to do.

To begin with, we must avoid being taken in by words. The C.N.E. is not a political association – that has always been its sincere intention – but none the less, even though its external action was the stubborn maintenance of the spirit of the Resistance against the nascent spirit of Vichy, it has not been able to prevent its internal history during these ten years from being a sort of confrontation between its Communist and its non-Communist members. This confrontation has always tried to be amicable, with the result that, over a certain period, if there have been among us members who were frankly anti-Communist, they have ended by leaving us. However, a friendly confrontation does not mean identity of views – quite the contrary: what makes our association thoroughly alive is our differences.

These differences, however, are never so great that they can endanger the essential thing – that is to say, the idea we all have of the future of Man. The Resistance bound us together, but what also keeps us together is a larger affinity: many members of the C.N.E. doubtless do not see in the social revolution which has conquered the world from the Elbe to the China Sea an example they desire to see victorious in France, but in any case none of them can tolerate the idea that anyone should wish to crush it where it exists. Anti-Communism which wishes for such a destruction is our common enemy.

This is why – and now I come back to my main subject, that is to say to the necessary criticism of our own thoughts and acts

– this is why the inquiry now being carried on in *Humanité* by our friend Pierre Courtade closely concerns us all. I personally can agree with almost everything he says. He advances, as a postulate, an indisputable fact. This revolution, extending from the Elbe to the China Sea, is the work of the Communists. In all the countries where the flag of Socialism flies, that is their work and no one else's. When, therefore, as at present, the Communists confront their thoughts with their actions, they have no lessons to receive from anyone, even over the errors they may have committed during this long struggle. And Pierre Courtade is a thousand times right when, speaking of the makers of sermons or epigrams, he writes: 'We have no accounts to render to those people.'

It is true. But there are also other people. There are their friends. And among their friends there are ourselves, the members of the Comité National des Ecrivains.

For the same Pierre Courtade, speaking of the errors committed, writes: *The abuses were at first imperceptible, and when they were noticed the evil had gone so deep that it was impossible, with circumstances as they were, to attack it without incurring a very grave risk for the revolution.* That is the crux. It is by reference to those words that we in turn shall be able to judge our own actions.

If I examine first – since this self-criticism must in all honesty begin with myself – what I have done during these ten years, I might at first sight find that I have not behaved too badly. It might seem to me – at first sight – that if the abuses, as Courtade says, were at first imperceptible, or in other words passed unnoticed, that was in any case not the fault of those men who kept repeating, as I did: 'Those who are fighting cannot always clearly distinguish how the battle is going. They are like Fabrice at Waterloo. The rôle of the writer, of the intellectual, is to march slightly on the flank, the better to discern the ambushes and to warn the fighters of them.' But that is what neither Courtade nor his friends were willing at that time to recognize. 'No,' they used to tell us, 'only those who are fighting can see clearly. It is in them that all reason and all truth are to be found. Separated from them, you are in the abstract, your problems are false problems, your worries false worries.' That is what I, in particular, was told at the time of the Rajk trial. 'Do you claim,' I was asked, 'to have more light on this trial than millions of Communists have?' Today Courtade writes: *It will now be necessary to find out how it was possible to rig this trial with such precision that it carried the conviction of all those who were present at it*. But when I tried to tell the Communists that for me and for some others what seemed to blaze out from this affair was, on the contrary, a set of contradictions so flagrant that in our eyes the whole trial could only be an immense lie, Aragon wrote that I was calling him a liar. The contrary was obviously the case: it was *to him* and to the millions of Communists that the lies had been told, and I was trying to tell him so, but he would not believe me. And what might – still at first sight – seem even graver is the fact that I quickly understood that I would have either to keep silent or to break with the Communists. I did not break with them, and I did not remain entirely silent, but at the same time I did not shout as loudly as I should have wished.

All this – at first sight – might lead our Communist friends to think that it is a way of suggesting: 'We told you so.' But, to begin with, that would be a sterile attitude, of a kind that has always seemed to me deeply distasteful. And in addition, it is not what I now think. For I think today that, if Pierre Courtade and his friends were morally wrong in being unwilling to listen to us, we were historically right in trusting them none the less; even if, by thus muting our fears, we muted also our duties. For while we none of us at that time knew the whole truth, it is today certain that any attempt at division coming from the West, even if it had been founded on all the morality in the world, could have only made things worse: either – if it had succeeded – it would have endangered peace together with Socialism, or – if it had failed – it would simply have helped those in power to check all opposition and so have retarded the return of justice.[1] I shall not claim that I had understood these things clearly from the time of the Rajk trial. I only did so much later, at the moment of the affair of Slansky and the Jewish

---

[1] Six months after this speech the Hungarian tragedy, alas, confirmed this analysis. See also the note on p. 30.

doctors, when *Pravda* and *Izvestia* began contradicting themselves. It was then that I wrote to Jean Cassou that a hidden
struggle was assuredly going on over there between certain
quasi-Fascist *cliques* and the true democrats, as happened in
France at the time of Dreyfus; and that to try and lump everybody together meant confusing the harmful and the just, the
Merciers and the Picquarts, the Henrys and the Scheurer-
Kestners,[1] in single blind reprobation. But from the first my
attitude had always been dictated by another motive: for
although I admit I was often strongly tempted to retire, in my
turn, to the Aventine, in order to keep my conscience clear by
loudly proclaiming my disagreement, I always resisted it
because I knew too well that one never stays long making
speeches on the Aventine, and that one very soon joins the
enemies of Rome, one very soon becomes the more or less
consenting quarry of the adversaries of the revolution. But if, for
these various reasons, we need not regret our attitude, that does
not mean that it exempts us from all reproach. It is not, in fact,
enough for Courtade to tell us that 'the evil had gone too deep
to be attacked without involving the revolution in too grave a
danger'. He must go further and ask himself how – through
what errors – one reaches that point.

For after all, why is it that 'the abuses were at first imperceptible'? Why were they able to increase so wildly before anyone
noticed? It is because, from that moment, nobody was allowed
to be in a position to give warning of those abuses, it is because,
in particular, the writers were not allowed to carry out their
duty as flank guards or scouts, the duty I should like to see
assigned to them in the political struggle. I remember Pierre
Hervé saying to me in a broadcast discussion: 'If you want to
be listened to, well, join our ranks.' 'But if we join them,' I said,
'we shall be like the others, we shall no longer see anything.'
'All right,' he said mockingly, 'stay by the roadside, it suits you
very well.'

The lesson, I think, is obvious. It has proved possible to
blind millions of Communists by means of lies, which were at
first imperceptible – to use Courtade's phrase – and then more

[1] Personalities in the Dreyfus case.

and more outrageous, because of this prejudice that only the fighters can see the battle as it is. I published not long ago a short novel about the deception of militants, how easy it is and what profound harm it does, and this, I am told, is making quite a sensation in Poland today. But its only effect here, at the time, was to draw down upon me bitter reproaches. Experience since then has been harsh – to put it mildly: the execution of an innocent person is as great a crime in Hungary as it is in America. And such crimes are even harder to bear when committed under a Socialist régime. Some, it is true, tell me: 'Rajk was guilty. His rehabilitation is only a political expedient.' I don't see the difference, even though it is less horrible to rehabilitate a guilty person then to hang an innocent one. For what about the lie? If they didn't lie yesterday, are they then lying to us today? And we can no longer pretend not to know. Must we in future, knowing that we are being lied to, always accept the lie without saying a word? Must we without a word watch these millions of trusting comrades being treated as minors? I shall not this evening repeat the prediction I have been making without cease for ten years: one day this trust will wake up in doubt and incredulity. And I leave to your imaginations the consequences of a decay like that.[1] It must not be possible for any Rajk affair to occur in future, now that no excuse, no blindness can any longer justify silence. The revolution is no longer in any danger of being crushed. The abscess has been lanced. I should, therefore, now like us to consider, with calmness, a revision of the statue – if I may use the term – of the progressive writer, and with it – this is the point I have been leading up to – that of the C.N.E., in relation to politics and to the revolutionary struggle. Because – as I said before – even though most of the members of the C.N.E. are not Communists, there is in any case not a single one among us who is fighting in the opposite camp. And so we can all be given a hearing as friends, even when we are expressing fears. And I even think that the lesson of events is that we *must* be given a hearing. At the time of the doctors' case I remember having

---

[1] Six months later the Hungarian insurrection provided a clear-cut image of this 'decay' also. See also the note on p. 28.

had an obstinate struggle to get the *Page du C.N.E.*, published at
that time in the *Lettres Françaises*, simply to mention that the
question would be debated. It will be remembered that, failing
this, I succeeded in preventing the C.N.E.'s page from appearing again. That removed an ambiguity, but it was also a confirmation that all we were allowed was silence. And today I am
wondering: do the reasons for that suppression still exist? If
there is a lesson from all this, should it not perhaps take just this
form: the return of the prodigal son – I mean, the reappearance
of a page, a free platform, in which the writers of the C.N.E.
would be authorized, not to indulge in recriminations about the
past, and still less, of course, in attacks on the Party, in demon-
strations of hostility, but to say what they think from day to
day and, if necessary, on occasion to make plain a doubt or
a disagreement. In short, to be heard by the militants, before
fresh 'at first imperceptible abuses', which will always tend to
arise, have succeeded in establishing themselves once more.
I will say frankly what I think. If an audience among the
militants were to continue to be refused to us, if we were forced
to remain always by the roadside which suits us very well, if
there were to be no change as though nothing had happened,
as though no innocent person had died, this would, I am afraid,
have an extremely grave significance. For after all, as one of my
Communist friends wrote to me by way of thanks and con-
gratulation: 'You were right and we were wrong, but in keeping
confidence in Us you were right where They were wrong.' *They*,
our adversaries, our enemies. But this keeping confidence would
deserve a different and much less flattering name, if the Communists were to prove *them* right today – those others who have
refused to trust them and have left them and fought against
them – and if they did not now repay our trust but instead
continued to say to us: 'Keep quiet!'

I do not mean that what I am asking for can come about
in a day. I am not ignorant of the hindrances that will need to
be conquered, the obstacles that will need to be surmounted.
I can gauge realistically all the reasons, moral and other, that
may make it difficult to resurrect a C.N.E. page. I hope at any
rate that the spirit of this hypothetical page will become that

of our association. I hope that the members of the C.N.E. will, from now on, do their job properly as attentive scouts. André Wurmser has often twitted me on my excessive taste for problems of conscience, on my tendency to see, in disquiet about matters of error and truth, justice and injustice, one of the most truly human functions of the human spirit. I don't know if these tastes still seem to him unreasonable. I hope not. I hope that to refuse to give way in future to any too facile confidence, to any too comfortable blindness will become the charter of all members of the C.N.E. Oh! it isn't easy, I have no illusions about that. It is simpler, much simpler, to struggle against Hitler than to struggle against comrades. I often said to myself, during the Resistance, that it was not difficult to resist in France. But in London, in the midst of intrigues and scandals, treacheries and stabs in the back, what would I have done? Would I have denounced all those discreditable things – at the risk of weakening Free France in her struggle against Nazi Germany? Or would I have passed them over in silence – at the risk of covering up lying and injustice? It is not so easy to answer. This helps us to understand – perhaps to approve – many of the silences there have been in the U.S.S.R. and elsewhere: to understand, even, that true courage sometimes consisted in keeping silence, in muzzling one's inner revolt or indignation. Yes, our rôle is a difficult one. But that is our honour also. Our honour lies in its demanding both such courage and such clear-sightedness – often not excluding grief and if need be, remorse. The hope I form with all my heart is that, in the new year which begins for the C.N.E. this evening, we may live up to this honour.

. . . . .

The whole speech was listened to with petrified attention. Not wishing that – breaking the established custom – a discussion should be opened on the presidential speech, I called on the secretary-general to speak next, without even giving the audience time to applaud, supposing it may have wished to do so. The rest of the meeting went forward normally.

But when 'miscellaneous business' was reached, several voices were raised, asking to return to my speech. I stuck to custom and did not open the debate. I would not reveal here what was said then – it should remain within those four walls – had not the discussion transgressed the rules and overflowed, if I may use the expression, into the domaine public. *A voice asked how, if there was no discussion, it would be possible to express agreement with my proposal. I said that members who wished to do so would be free to inform the Secretariat. But thereupon, intervening unexpectedly, the editor of* Les Lettres Françaises *told the meeting that this would be a waste of time, even if the decision were unanimous: he, and he alone, was master of his paper, and he would not reopen its pages to the C.N.E.: he had, he said, succeeded in 'depoliticizing' it and had no intention of letting it be 'repoliticized'. He ended, there was a silence, and that was all. And the meeting went on to other business.*

According to a custom which dated from the foundation of the C.N.E., the presidential speeches were always published immediately in the Lettres Françaises. *Without indulging in any illusion, I gave its staff time to ask me for my text. But, as may be expected, the telephone did not ring. I then suggested to a friendly paper that it should publish it. The suggestion was accepted and the text sent off. Then I heard nothing. A week passed, then another (I came to Paris once a week). I received neither a refusal nor a firm assurance of any publication date. I decided then to send a copy to all the members of the C.N.E. (only a quarter or a third of whom had been present at the meeting) with a covering letter making these points:*

'It seems to me indispensable to know, once for all, what sort of association your president is presiding over. Perhaps he has been wrong during all these years in believing that it claimed kinship, above all, with the great tradition of Zola. If this is not, or no longer, the case, if the majority of us think that in certain circumstances we ought politely to beg Zola to hold his peace, it would be as well for your president to be informed of his mistake.

'For this reason I should be greatly interested in knowing your opinion, if you would be kind enough to express it.'

But the letter and the speech remained with the printer, for a few days later the daily paper in question made me a most attractive suggestion: that it should start the C.N.E. page in its own columns. It would be necessary, however, to prevent this from appearing as a hostile act towards Les Lettres Françaises. *Or, for the same reason, as a direct consequence of my speech. It would be best, therefore, that I should draw up another text, a sort of appeal, which would serve, in fact, as the inaugural page.*

I set to work, but by the time I had finished I was no longer president of the C.N.E.

A conflict between the editor of the Lettres Françaises *and a member of his staff (both of them members of the executive committee of the C.N.E.) had obliged me, rather unwillingly, to intervene. This intervention had caused a resignation, followed the next day by another, and this rendered the situation completely absurd: because four years earlier I had, in the end and with the utmost reluctance, accepted the presidency only as a result of the obstinate insistence of the two members now resigning – in order, they said to me then, to save the C.N.E. and its unity. If, I wrote to them, they now no longer wanted to save it, what was I doing in this outfit? Besides, our quarrel, though it had broken out over a straw, was none the less a perfectly clear issue:*

'I wanted to open a breach in the wall of silence which you (the Communists) have had built up between you and us ever since these terrible events. If the C.N.E. can bring itself to sleep in the shadow of that wall, why then let it, if it is sleepy. I cannot – and even less without you.'

It was, therefore, as 'honorary president' (Francis Jourdain, after a long resistance, had agreed to succeed me) that I now addressed myself to my colleagues in the C.N.E.:

Since these lines are addressed, more than to anyone else, to the members of the Comité National des Ecrivains, it is necessary that I should first announce here a very commonplace piece of news: a few days ago I gave up the presidency of that body.

There is, I hasten to say, no connexion between this very

small event and the lines which follow: and I have thought it right to make this statement in the first place out of simple honesty, in order that my colleagues may not think I am still addressing them *ex officio*, but also, and chiefly, to prevent any interpretation damaging to the C.N.E. Our adversaries are very clever at taking advantage of the slightest sign of dispute in order to envenom it into a quarrel: I shall not fall into that trap.

Let me then make it clear – it will be sufficient – that rightly or wrongly I raised at a meeting of our executive committee a question which seemed inopportune enough to two of its leading members to provoke their immediate resignation. Since I was neither disposed to retract nor to be the cause of a split within the C.N.E., I resigned the chair, to be able to invite the two resigning members to return – if, as I hope, they wish to do so; and in order that this seat might be occupied by a more equable president, one better able to conciliate and to exercise his arbitral rôle with serenity.

.   .   .   .   .

For I must admit I can no longer be serene. Our association has always claimed kinship with a great example, that of Emile Zola. One cannot both claim kinship with a great example and reserve the right to forget it whenever following it becomes embarrassing. When it is a question of the Rosenbergs, it is easy for progressive writers to vent their indignation. For they know *who* and what immense social injustice is the gainer from that sort of crime. But when an innocent man is hanged in a Socialist country, it is much more difficult to intervene. Infinitely more difficult, and more painful. In the first place because, they tell themselves, it is after all not 'the same thing'; no repression in a Socialist country has ever struck any but men accused of betraying the Revolution; it is horrible, if they have not betrayed it, to have hanged them; but would not accusing the Revolutionary power before world opinion weaken the Revolution – that is to say, betray it even more gravely? What then, in this dilemma, would have been the way shown by Zola? What would he have done?

I can only, of course, answer on my own account. When Rajk was condemned and I was forced, as I read the trial, to realize that it contained so many incredible contradictions, I wished to set progressive opinion on its guard, to ask it to become as uneasy as I was and perhaps to protest, to demand at least some light; the answer I received was that I was treating the Communists as liars. Of course, it was to *them* that the lies had been told, and atrocious lies – to millions of trusting men. I am recalling this, believe me, not out of vanity, nor to crow over anybody. To begin with, what right would I have? For, when I was told 'trust us or break with us' – well, I kept silence. I was sick at heart, and not speaking did not mean not thinking, but I kept silence. To begin with, because the example of those who, strong in their sense of righteousness and good conscience, were crying out all the time, was there to restrain me: for I could hear their voices combining in the vast croaking of the counter-revolution. The purest of those voices (I am thinking of Bourdet's, of Camus's) were no longer distinguishable, in that din, from those of the crows. Everyone was shouting 'Justice!' and protecting, even if unwillingly, a world of injustices. Faced with the choice of crying with the birds of prey or keeping silence, I chose silence. It has lasted seven years: seven years during which I have written practically nothing but my books. I went on, of course, with the struggle for peace and for the memory of the Resistance, but with that weight on my tongue. I can truly claim that this seven years' silence is being broken publicly today for the first time.

This will remind some of you of the story of the Pope's mule[1] which silently champed its bit for seven years, but then found relief in such a magnificent kick that of the young page, its former tormentor, all that remained was some vague, pale yellow dust in the Avignon sky. Yet there is a great difference between that mule and me: during seven years I have nourished not rancour but hope. I have never ceased hoping that in the end the right to speak would be restored to me. And so this is a great day, because the thing has actually happened.

Perhaps not in the place I would have expected or hoped for.

[1] A story by Alphonse Daudet.

But whatever the place, I am now being asked not to be silent but to speak, to say what has been weighing on my heart for seven years. My friends, this right of speech is being given to us all. But the present declaration would be decidedly useless if it were not soon followed by yours. At our general meeting, I made a speech which now, after my resignation, smells somewhat of the last will and testament. In it I expressed the hope of seeing reappear that *Page du C.N.E.*, which at a certain moment was forced to scuttle itself in order to prevent ambiguity (we had thought we were free there and we were not). That page – and you with it – had withdrawn into silence, a silence we were not in a position to break without going over to the enemy. Some did go over. We did not. That is why today the right to make ourselves heard cannot be denied us. The platform I am inaugurating today is the recognition of this right.

And it is not only a right: it is a duty. For there has been only one excuse for our silences: that they were imposed on us. But they could be imposed on us because we allowed our dilemma to grow, until it grew to be terribly simple: either to go over to the enemy or to keep quiet. 'Grew to be,' I said. For it was not always so. Indeed it would never have been so if, when we decided to cry out, it had not been already too late. Yes: we have paid heavily for having awakened too late: we have spent too long in arguing about our rôle. Have I not repeated often enough (but people refused to listen to me) that the rôle of a writer in a revolution is, first and foremost, to keep watch? If the writer does not, at the first alert, denounce the excesses of power, who will ever denounce them? For the very nature of power implies power to misuse it; and the temptation of all officialdom is to truckle to the powers that be. No constitution has ever been able, by itself, to master all the excesses of power; as for the Soviet constitution, of whose existence they are now reminding us by recalling it to life, where has it been all these years? The *only* bridle, when power blinds a too trusting people, is Emile Zola. Yes, I know – I have said so already – it is much easier to be an Emile Zola against the sword and the mitre than against a revolutionary tribunal. In the first case, all one risks is a *bourgeois* prison. In the second, the risk is that of being treated as an enemy of the people and even – still graver – of becoming one. But at the same time, does not the honour of us writers consist in risking *all*, even our souls? Do not misunderstand me: there are ignoble risks in which the soul is lost ignobly. I do not mean them: I mean those infinitely noble risks which a man accepts for the greater glory of mankind, even if all he stands to gain is oblivion, or worse.

It is in this spirit, I think, that this platform is made available to us. To say here anything and everything – no: our adversaries would make short work of entangling us in sophisms under the guise of liberty. But to express a doubt, a warning or a cry of alarm: that is our sphere. Without forcing ourselves, of course! It may happen that for months on end we shall need to express no more than quite restful ideas. I think, on the occasion of this birth (or rebirth), an editorial committee should be formed to take charge of the page. I shall not be able to sit on it: after my resignation, that might lead to false interpretations. But I shall be at its disposal, of course, as much as it wishes. Being again, as formerly, a member of the C.N.E. without title or office, I hereby call my fellow-writers to this necessary task.

But I waited in vain for publication. The petard, which had been damp for a long time, was unprimed. I was hardly, if at all, surprised. Anything was possible immediately after the Twentieth Congress, when disarray in people's minds had not yet solidified into positions that were all the more firm and intransigent the deeper the cracks which they covered. Two months had gone by, and it was too late – on this point the game was decided: nothing would happen, there would be no C.N.E. page, either in Lettres Françaises *or elsewhere. And the C.N.E. itself would give itself over to sleep – until what awakening?*

Besides, it was the holidays. Things were calming down, it seemed. A few rumblings still arose from the Vistula or the Danube, that was all. . . . They broke out, when autumn came, into the clamours of insurrection.

The Soviet intervention in Hungary produced in the C.N.E. the expected storm. In May people had found me too bold to follow; in November I was considered too restrained. Those who had turned a deaf ear now called on me to decide: revolt or dissidence!

Let someone else, *I answered*, lead the rebellion. I no longer feel I enjoy the confidence which I thought I still enjoyed last May on the part of a large number of members. But as soon as Aragon raised his voice everyone scurried underground. At the same time you will understand that I am also not much attracted by the idea of limping after the very people who deserted me in the past (whispering their approval in private, but doing no more). And to be perfectly frank, I cannot see why they should be more determined today, unless we join in the hue and cry – which I should not find to my taste either.

However, an extraordinary general meeting was called. It took place six weeks later, on 13 January. Excitement had somewhat calmed down. In the meantime the executive committee had, for the first time since its foundation, made a direct approach to a Socialist Government in order to defend writers gravely menaced by a repression which seemed likely to be big with injustices, as all repressions are. The majority of the members of the association seemed satisfied with this demonstration; a minority remained reticent; a small and very hostile group apparently intended to come to the meeting for the last time, merely in order to resign with éclat. It was to that minority and that group that I addressed the following speech:

For four years I was your president. I have ceased to be so, discreetly, in consequence – whether direct or indirect does not much matter – of my last presidential speech. Today you know (if you have looked at your voting papers) that I no longer wish, for the moment, to retain any part in the actual direction.

At the risk of seeming to attach too much importance to my own personal actions, I must, in order to make myself clear, remind you of some of them since I joined the C.N.E. at the Liberation.

I came into it, like all of you, to safeguard the essence of that which brought together in the Resistance writers whose ideas were often extremely opposed, but who were united about certain fundamental principles which, it seemed to me, could not be questioned by any of us.

I was obliged, quite soon, to realize that even these fundamental principles were not accepted in everybody's mind in the
same way. I was obliged, quite soon, to take up my own personal
position on this matter in public in order to avoid any
ambiguity.

One of these principles for which I have fought unceasingly
for the last twelve years is the unconditional respect due to the
truth. People have often written or thought that in doing so
I was fighting for a moral principle. That is also true, but for
me it was far from being the strongest motive. Lying has always
seemed to me not so much immoral as destructive. Ten years
ago I declared, in *L'Heure du Choix*, that if the confidence of the
people is misled, this will rot away their Socialist faith and, on
the day of awakening, will lead them to despair – make of them
an easy victim for the worst reaction. I am recalling this, in the
light of Budapest, not in order to boast of my clear-sightedness,
but to add that it is also ten years that I have been imprisoned
in the dilemma: either to keep my worries to myself, or to
publish them in the adversaries' Press, and thereby to lend
support to other lies.

I preferred to believe that, after the terrible revelations,
which went beyond what I myself had feared, after it had
turned out that those who thought they were preventing me
from propagating calumnies were covering up crimes, the right
to speak out would be restored to me – that it would be offered
to us all. I said so in the speech which turned out to be the last
of my presidency; for I was forced to understand that people
felt more alarm than regret, and were much more apprehensive
of the effects of so black a truth on popular opinion than anxious
to draw from it its severe conclusions. Two months of efforts to
break down this fresh wall, to find the chink in the armour
which had been buckled on again, have resulted only in my
failure and a fresh silence.

For a long time, none the less, I hoped that it would perhaps
suffice to show patience: though foreseeing once more, and
once more saying in vain, that if people waited too long the
result would be that, by dint of trying to sit on all these safety
valves, they would produce a more violent explosion. Some

friends of mine from Eastern Germany – Communist friends
from out there – have told me this anecdote, which is going the
rounds of East Berlin. The new schoolmaster notices that his
young pupils have got it firmly lodged in their heads that twice
two is nine. Indignantly he goes and tells the mayor, a party
official. But he is told: 'Don't go too fast, though. Don't hustle
them. Twice two is eight . . . twice two is seven. . . .' And, of
course, hardly has he begun when already his pupils are
scribbling on all the walls that twice two makes two, makes one,
makes nought. . . . When, after years of lies, truth emerges on
the rim of its well, the worst policy of all is to try and modestly
cover it up: it must be honestly helped to step out of its well, or
else thrown back to the bottom again and buried under fresh
stones, provided one has the strength.

As you see, I am not playing the moralist, the redresser of
wrongs, as I have been accused of doing for ten years *ad nauseam*.
The reply has come, alas, dramatically, in the form of very real,
very practical, very political and, lastly, very bloody consequences. It is not only morality that is suffering; the harshest
blows have fallen and are still falling upon Socialism, upon the
future of Socialism, the faith of peoples in Socialism, the faith
of a whole young generation educated to Socialism – harsher
blows in a few months than in all these last twelve years. Could
a virile and responsible C.N.E. have done something to prevent
this? Yes, I believe it could. From its past prestige it still had an
influence which we might have brought into play. We have
seen this clearly on the occasion of the still very modest, but
perhaps effective, approach we have made to the Budapest
Government for the safeguarding of the Hungarian writers. Is
this the beginning of a change in the attitude of the C.N.E.
towards the dangers which truth and, with it, justice, men's
liberty and the liberty of their thought are running daily in the
world? Or is it merely an isolated start, perhaps even a feint for
the purpose of returning as quickly as possible to our indifference? For, during the last five or six years, the C.N.E. has
become more and more emasculated in the hope of avoiding
trouble. I am not accusing it, I too am responsible for this
emasculation, having been unable to prevent it. I was unable

to prevent it, but I can no longer submit to it. If it is to go on, if the C.N.E. can really survive only by resuming or continuing this eunuch existence, it has really no need of me.

I shall not, however, leave the C.N.E. I hope I shall never leave it. In the first place, out of loyalty to the memory, the friendships built up in the struggle in the old days. But chiefly for the sake of being there, of being in its ranks on the day it wakes up. For in spite of everything I believe it will wake up. I hope, failing proof to the contrary, that its action in defence of the Hungarian writers is a beginning and not a feint, a timid beginning but still a beginning of rebirth. Yet I think also that most of our people – to be frank with you, the majority of our members – are not in favour of such a change. This has been made clear to me. I think this violent reversal of our immobility, the only one for a long time, has been due to the weight of a minority, whose opinion silently made itself heard, for once, with sufficient power. I therefore think also that this minority, if it means to promote the rebirth which is taking shape, will have to regroup, to become self-conscious and perhaps to constitute within the C.N.E. a kind of 'Her Majesty's Opposition', determined to prevent a return to the practices of hibernation. An opposition like the one that has never broken the unity of the United Kingdom and yet has to be reckoned with: one that, in our case, will prevent this Oblomov from going back to the sofa, or back to apathy, and will force it to fight for the truth as it once did, even though, year after year, it has forgotten that it was made for precisely that. And it is for this reason that I want, with that day in view, to be free – a simple citizen of the C.N.E. This is why I am not standing for election again: and why, as my first act of opposition, I shall not take part in the election which is about to be held.

I cannot in fact see any other way of demonstrating my disagreement with our complacency, except to abstain openly in this election. For I object, at the same time, to there being any personal discrimination, I object to the striking out of names – which can only mean unpleasant aspersions on individuals – when we are all of us simultaneously responsible for what we have all of us become. I shall not therefore at any price vote, or seem to call upon others to vote, against our friends on the committee; but neither will I vote or call for a vote in favour of a pure and simple re-election as though everything were for the best in the best of all possible C.N.E.s, because, if I did so, I should have the impression that we were once more allowing ourselves our annual dose of sleeping-pills. For these reasons I shall abstain.

But to those of us who are perhaps thinking of a still stronger opposition, I repeat with insistence: do not leave the C.N.E.! Even if shortly you find yourselves in disagreement with it, say so publicly if you wish, but do not walk out! It is within it that the spark will kindle, if it is going to kindle; not outside, not among its adversaries. On the contrary, on the day when something happens here – perhaps few will have wanted it, but they will have wanted it with decision – it will be our prodigal colleagues (the ones who left the C.N.E. to injure it instead of remaining to act within it as I begged them to do with all my strength), it will be they who will then probably regret their sterile absence and perhaps ask us to let them come back. As you see, I am optimistic. I believe in a C.N.E. not renewed but recovered, and above all retempered. Because it is always in the actual ordeal that all human things are tempered anew.

.   .   .   .   .

In the debate that followed there were several violent clashes, but when it came to the voting I was the only one to abstain, and the executive committee received a unanimous vote. (Two or three members, however, handed in their resignation a few days later.) There were, none the less, signs that an 'active minority' intended to form itself into a group. Its first chance of demonstrating its existence was when it took to the Hungarian Legation a protest in the name of 'members of the C.N.E.' against the suspension of the Hungarian Writers' Union. Then I went abroad. Not long after my return, the arrest of two great writers at Budapest seemed to me to face this minority with the occasion and duty of demonstrating again. I suggested that all those who had, in one way or another, assured me that they shared my views, should sign a telegram of protest to the Hungarian Government, and another, couched as an appeal, to the writers of the Soviet Union. But several of my corre-spondents, who were members of the executive committee, asked me to give that committee a chance of enlisting the weight of the C.N.E. as a whole. I consented – though without any illusion; as I expected, what had been a firm protest was there reduced to a mere request for elucidation. What was more, Francis Jourdain, the president, forwarded to me the 'friendly reproach' of the members of the executive committee for having tried to take action over their heads. Here is my reply:

4 May 1957

Thank you for your kind note, so affectionate for all its severity. 'Severe but just?' I wonder. You see, I should like you to remind the executive committee of certain facts about the past which it seems to have forgotten. I was its president for four years, and I shared with it a heavy responsibility, while stifling my own scruples out of solidarity. Then came the time when I thought I was authorized (as a result of revelations which showed we had been very wrong) to ask that I should be repaid in kind. The same solidarity was – in the nicest possible way – refused to me. This, you will agree, should more than restore to me my liberty. Persistence in a recognized error has always seemed to me the worst attitude of all. I gave warning of the danger that threatened the C.N.E. when some new affair should arise. It was not long before Budapest made the threat a reality. Like many others, I was tempted to leave. I would have done so, had I not known that the C.N.E. still has a certain prestige in the countries of Eastern Europe and that, in the present circumstances, this prestige is double-edged: for, thanks, to it, the C.N.E. can encourage errors by its silence just as much as it can restrain them by its protests. That is why, with all my strength, I restrained those who wanted to walk out, by promis-ing them that we should together constitute that 'Her Majesty's Opposition' which I had proposed openly and clearly at our general meeting. For I hope that you will at least do me the justice of recognizing that I do nothing underhand, that on the contrary I always announce what I am going to do and why I am going to do it. Now I am bound by my promise: those whom I held back have the right to demand that I keep it.

Well, it does not consist in going on playing the petty game of anodyne votes, 'requests for elucidation', or questions about the fate of so-and-so, forwarding these periodically to a government whose silence has already struck us on the right cheek and on the left and given us a kick on the right buttock (and I admit that I personally am sensitive in that quarter and feel no masochistic desire to balance it with the left side). My promise of an 'active minority' means action – and if the executive committee wishes to take action with us, we shall obviously be sincerely delighted. That is why I agreed that it should be informed of my plan, although I was not willing myself to inform it. I was wrong, however, for what I feared has happened. The executive committee has sent its *nth* 'request for elucidation' and nullified our firm protest – has once more, however involuntarily, cut the grass from under our feet, or, if you prefer it, bitched us. I am not surprised at the reaction of the executive committee towards me. It is very natural. It is no good warning people that one is going to make a damn nuisance of oneself; when one really does it one must expect disapproval. I could also understand perfectly well if the executive committee refused to let me repeat the offence. That if I should continue to use, without prior reference to it, my titles as member of the C.N.E. and honorary president, it might consider it necessary to deprive me of them. You can assure our friends that I shall have no hard feelings. I merely think that they would be wrong. I am convinced that our active minority is 'safeguarding the future' (to use the term chosen by its executive committee), in the same way as the declarations of this Labour member or that ex-minister in protest against the Suez attack have safeguarded the future of Great Britain in the eyes of the Arab populations; or in the same way that a French Socialist who protests against the present policy at the risk of being excluded from his Party is also safeguarding the future of his Party in France and the future of France in Algeria.

This does not mean that I intend to oppose for the fun of opposing. Every time a problem arises that does not threaten to set the members of the executive committee ineluctably against one another, and so to reduce them either to silence or to 'requests for elucidation', you may be sure I shall take part in the debates with the same pleasure and zeal as before. But in other cases, in those cases where a negative result is a fore-gone conclusion, I shall be obliged to conform to the promises I have given to friends whom I kept back from leaving us only by committing myself to act as I am doing.

I am making life difficult for you, and towards you personally I feel an affection that is both tender and remorseful. I cannot forget how you struggled all night to refuse the presidency, nor how, when morning came, instead of sounding the trumpet to rescue you, I helped the wolf through my insistence. And when I did so I knew that, by the force of circumstances, I was bound to make a damned nuisance of myself and that you would be the first victim of my pranks. I think, whatever happens, you are fond enough of me to forgive me, just as you are sure that my affection will always be deeply loyal to you.

V.

Not long after this statement, in which I recalled my implicit commitment towards an 'active minority' which I still hoped to animate, the ordinary general meeting proceeded to the annual election of its executive committee. I was not present. As the result of this assembly, Aragon was nominated president.

Two years earlier I should have rejoiced profoundly at this election. I had at that time proposed that the presidency should thenceforward be statutorily limited to two years (I had occupied it for that period). It would thus have been possible to remedy a major anomaly: why had not the C.N.E. ever managed to have as its president the writer most obviously marked out by his reputation and his quality for this honour? Because it was thought that, the majority of its members not being Communists, a Communist president, and one who was so conspicuous, would have 'compromised' them. An obligatory change every two years, by making 'rotation' automatic, would, so I argued, have reduced such a fear to nothing. But my proposal was rejected, and I was once more, in spite of myself, kept in office.

But while at that time the election of Aragon to the presidency would have been obviously a simple decency, it now no less evidently acquired, after my attempts to reform the C.N.E., actually in opposition to him – and ignoring the considerations which, for twelve years, had prevented this election – a totally different significance: that of an overt rallying – to an individual, certainly, but mainly to a line of conduct. As long as the C.N.E. had retained, in the person of Francis Jourdain, a president who played his part as an arbiter between two opposing tendencies, the external action of an 'active minority' still had some practical value; it prevented the C.N.E. as a whole from being automatically confused with the action – or inaction – of the majority group.

By crossing the line and taking as its president the illustrious protagonist of that very tendency, the assembly knew that it was knocking on the head any effective minority efforts: in fact, whatever this minority might do, who could any longer imagine the C.N.E. in any guise except that of the writer whom it had just, in the most public way possible, called upon to lead it? Once again, the cards had been played, and there was now no possible hope that the calculated ambiguity of an 'active opposition' could preserve for the C.N.E. the benefit of the doubt, either in France or abroad.

The C.N.E. was in fact openly ratifying, for instance in the eyes of the Hungarian Government, and openly claiming as its own, an attitude and an ethic that were precisely the opposite of those which formerly produced an Emile Zola and a Romain Rolland. They could not possibly be mine. I must sadly make up my mind to keep aloof from the C.N.E., unequivocally, in my turn.

·   ·   ·   ·   ·

And so today there is in France no literary association defending what the writers of the Resistance together defended.

The dissidents in the *Union pour la Verité* defend neither union (since they are dissident) nor truth (since they have still only denounced the lies of one side).[1] What they are defending really is a policy; one of whose primary objects, openly admitted indeed, is the destruction of the C.N.E.

They have no more valuable auxiliary than the C.N.E. itself as it has now become. And so we have, at one end, this

---

[1] Since these lines were written, I am happy to be able to pay homage to their president, Louis Martin-Chauffier, who (though in a different capacity) has denounced in *Le Figaro*, in bold though measured terms, the camps, repression and tortures in Algeria.

paralytic C.N.E., and at the other end an anti-C.N.E. in its image. Between the two there is now no longer anything.

As far as I am concerned, both sides have shut me up so completely that it is no longer a question of my holding my tongue but of not having a tongue at all.

Must I then throw the helve after the hatchet? My answer, no less firmly, is 'No'. And on this point, here is my concluding song.

The Lay, or Bequests, of Bruller, alias Vercors

> In the year nineteen fifty-seven
> I, Bruller, writing as Vercors,
> hereby declare it vain and more
> to build an aisle to squeeze the nave in
> or barrels in a garret store,
> and plain as two and two make four
> a man should either sound his note
> boldly on, or rest his throat.
>
> So in that year which I have said,
> in August, sweetest month of all
> when poplars in the breeze are swayed
> and vine-creepers clothe the house wall,
> desire came over me, to split
> the silence of imprisonment,
> to which my reason gave consent
> too long not to be shamed by it.
>
> If I would save one farthing still,
> I think it best no one should see me.
> Good-bye! I'm off to the old mill:
> for not a soul will either free me
> to speak my mind, or even see me
> go. So I smother my complaints
> (my doom, to be a quilled and reamy
> martyr, one of the writer saints).
>
> .   .   .   .   .   .
>
> First, in the C.N.E. I leave
> others to do what I but tried.

I hope to this day and believe
the thing may yet come from inside.
But perhaps not. I fear, in that case,
the occasion for it will betide
my lords and masters off their stride,
and they expect it not in that place.

Will come as on the mice the cat,
who leisuredly prepares his spring
(Hitler's already shown us that),
so delicately manœuvring
that the good parliament lets us fall
one by one in the subtle trap,
till the matured decisive rap
hooks the Republic in fast thrall.

Will hook and hold you all, good lords,
and make you swallow your true words,
in one dishonour sink together,
unless you allow, honestly,
your Union for Truth to gather
within this stubborn C.N.E.
– Aragon with Martin-Chauffier,
Sartre beside Stanislas Fumet.

Item, to them this earnest word:
not in sweet dreams to lie too long.
They must in good time rise up strong,
some to see that the truth be heard,
others that cant shall lack reporters.
So they together shall march out
elbow to elbow and put to rout
the shadow of police headquarters.

Item, I leave to all mankind
who love justice and liberty
(while they remain still of sound mind)
to fight against adversity
on the side of the working class,
for it will still be, as it was,
the first to awaken. This I hope
– or misery will have dread scope.

D

Item, to all my friends I leave
my confidence in victory.
Neither in my style's vanity
contained, nor strained through the words' sieve,
but face to face with harsh reverses
– soon or late, and not half and half –
and not in any threadbare verses,
it shines in your united strife.

Finally, sitting here at day's
end, all alone, remote, yet well
in body, well in my soul's core,
dictating these bequests and lays,
I see my purpose, and will tell:
As in the old Resistance days,
to fan your hope to a fresh blaze
is the burden of that pest, Vercors.
Amen.

2

Welcomed by All, Rebuffed by Everyone

OR AN INTERRUPTED DIALOGUE

*T*HROUGHOUT *these last years the greater part of my activity –*
apart from art and literature – has been devoted to one effort: to
helping the pursuit, or re-establishment, of the dialogue, or
genuine discussion, between the Communists and the rest, and in particular
between the French writers and those of the U.S.S.R.
    This effort has chiefly consisted in a great many attempts at clearing
up confusion. I strongly believe that it is no good trying to establish a
discussion between people who have not, to begin with, reached agreement
at least on some ideas, or rather on some principles. What will be found
in these pages is the dossier *of my attempts at getting this necessity*
admitted. And of how, from the Soviet side, they met with two failures.
The first was due perhaps to a slightly premature attempt. The second,
I am afraid, to more serious causes. But the two together deprived me,
from now on, of any power – or rather, I might say, any mandate – to
continue the effort.

.   .   .   .   .

    I was filled with high hopes, however, when on a visit to the
U.S.S.R. in July 1955 *I was asked for two articles: one of them*
was to be 'My Profession of Faith' – I wrote it on the spot, it
appeared in the Literaturnaya Gazeta *in Moscow while I was*
still there – uncut and unaltered. The other was to be on 'The Problems
of French Writers', for the review called Foreign Literature *which*
was just being started, and to which it would have been one of the
first French contributions. But this second article did not appear, for
reasons and in circumstances which will be explained later.

The *Literatournaya Gazeta* is doing me a great honour in asking me to contribute to it 'My Profession of Faith'. And I have, of course, eagerly consented.

But as I take up the pen, I feel a certain embarrassment. Some of us French writers find ourselves in a rather paradoxical situation. America publishes our books, but refuses to let us go there; the Soviet Union on the other hand invites and welcomes us with a warmth and friendship that go straight to our heart, but our works are not published there. And so we are, so to speak, cut in two: on the one side, the man; on the other, the writer. And I wonder from which of these two Vercors an answer is expected. If the writer, what credit can his literary ideas have with Soviet readers, who have not yet read a word of his? Will not these ideas, without the support of my books, appear hollow and displeasing – and if they displease, will they not harm my books? . . . Cruel dilemma for a writer![1]

But so be it. As we say in France, 'I'm not going to funk it'. I am all the more bound to this refusal because one of the first articles of faith in my profession as a writer is that we must, before everything else, be courageous, and dare to say what we think in all circumstances, whatever the cost of our frankness. A man who dares not risk displeasing is no true writer. This is enough to oblige me to answer without any concealment.

Let us begin at the beginning. As soon as he starts to write, a writer ought to ask himself a grave question: 'Why am I writing?' If they were frank with themselves they would answer, some of them: 'for the sake of glory', others: 'to earn my living' (and all these are hardly needed, they would be more useful in the fields or in a factory); yet others: 'to make my ideas prevail', or: 'to reform men's conduct', or: 'to depict reality', or: 'to educate my readers, or to direct them or to correct them'; or again: 'for no reason, simply to exercise

---

[1] Since then, many living French writers of all sorts of political tendencies have been translated in the U.S.S.R. So have this author's *Borderline* and *Put Out The Light*.

myself in thinking', or: 'to change society, take part in the struggle against its enemies', etc. etc.

When I ask myself that question, the answer I give myself, as far as I am concerned – and I think it is a sincere one, because my career as a writer only began rather late – is this: 'I write to expose lies and injustices. And I write also to try and help my readers to find the meaning of their life.'

The first of these two reasons for writing is easily understood. In the country where I live, it is extremely necessary; but there is none in which it is useless. In France it takes its place in the long tradition that runs from Voltaire exposing the Calas affair, to Victor Hugo exposing the crimes of Napoleon III, and to Zola exposing the Dreyfus affair. It was within this tradition that I began to write under the Occupation and that in the Resistance, I founded the *Editions de Minuit*, in order to expose the lies and criminal injustices of Vichy, to set French opinion on the alert against the atrocities that were being committed against the Communists, the Jews and all the victims of Nazism. I went on after the Liberation, together with many other French writers, indefatigably denouncing the war in Indo-China, the iniquitous verdicts against Henri Martin and the crime against the Rosenbergs; fighting against the rebirth of a German army; and demanding the liberation of Jacques Duclos and his fellow prisoners. But there is a more awkward duty: this arises when some lie or injustice seems to come from the camp of one's own friends. Then it takes much more courage to speak out. Yet there have been cases where I have done so – it was painful to me, but I do not regret it, for events since then have confirmed me in my belief that silence prolongs the evil instead of stifling it, whereas open discussion would have shortened its days.

My second reason for writing requires more explanation. It may seem rather vain to aim at 'helping one's readers to find the meaning of their lives'. It may seem even vainer under a Socialist régime, where the meaning of life emerges with clarity. But there are other problems besides the social ones, besides those of the human community. There are all those problems set by life to human beings, whatever their country and the

social régime under which they live, all those sorrows to which
innocent people are subject – the death of dear ones, a child's
sickness, old age, unhappy love, all those testing times in which
doubt and weariness of living seize hold on you. The best of
political régimes is still powerless to conquer, to justify or to
explain away such hardships. And a literature that pretended
they did not exist would be, in my eyes, neither complete nor
realistic. This is why, in my literary work, I try to mingle these
problems with the social problems, just as they are mingled in
real life.

I attempt something else which is more important still, and
which I will try to express. The human species is divided. It is
divided spiritually, politically and morally. One can, of course,
hope that it will cease to be so, but this for the time being is
what is called wishful thinking – that is to say a hope with no
chance of being realized in the immediate future. And the only
choice for our world of today is between two things: war and
co-existence. But there are two kinds of co-existence. The first
is the hostile co-existence of two opposed worlds, determined to
have no relations with each other. I have been struggling for
a very long time against that formula, which not only cannot
help leading to war, but impoverishes each half of the world by
depriving it of the wealth of the other half, and first and foremost of its cultural wealth. The only co-existence acceptable to
my way of thinking is the willing conciliation which allows of
the establishment of sincere relations so that the two parties may
enrich one another. In the cultural field, this requires that a
genuine dialogue be set going between all the forms of thought,
even if they are opposed, even if they seem mutually exclusive.

But this at once raises the first question, which is: 'Is such
a dialogue possible?'

The aim of all that I have written for the last five or six
years has been to show that, in spite of opposing points of view
which may seem irreconcilable, this dialogue is perfectly possible. To show that the disagreements are not as radical as they
may seem. *'Celui qui croyait au ciel, celui qui n'y croyait pas'*,[1]
Aragon has written in an unforgettable poem. Face to face with

---

[1] 'He who believed in heaven, he who did not believe.'

an extreme danger which menaced the whole human race, face to face with the mortal danger of Nazism, believers, Liberals and Communists saw their disagreements vanish and their divergencies come together, that they might save a thing of value which was common to them all: the human person. At that time they did not need to verify the fact that they had, at the bottom of their hearts, a similar idea of the 'person', more powerful than their disharmonies: danger and the enemy were there to show them this. But since the defeat of Nazism the disharmonies have come to the top again. What is needed now is to show that that agreement was not accidental, that that basic idea of what is *human* – and what is the essential – has not disappeared along with the fight, that it remains indestructible, and that that alliance of *celui qui croit au ciel* with *celui qui n'y croit pas* can flourish in time of peace as much as in war. Communist thinking conceives man from a materialist and historical viewpoint. Western thinking, which is still first and foremost Christian, conceives that same mankind in accordance with idealistic premises, with a divine revelation. It may seem that these two ways of thinking will never be able to come to agreement on basic ideas so contrary, and that any dialogue between them is doomed to remain sterile. I try to show that, in spite of this appearance, these opposed ideas converge upon an idea which *goes further back than either* – to show that Liberal Christians and Communists fought together against Nazism because of this common idea, even if neither of them had at that time become clearly conscious of it. In *Plus ou moins Homme*, *La Puissance du Jour, Les Animaux Dénaturés*, and the novel I am now finishing, this is the idea I have been trying to bring to light. For I am convinced that it is indispensable to the opening of a fruitful dialogue.

This does not mean that, in the course of such a dialogue, agreement would be obligatory. On the contrary: as we all agreed the other day, in that warm and friendly conversation which I had with the editorial staff of the *Literaturnaya Gazeta*, nothing is more fruitful than disagreements. One only becomes fully aware of what one thinks oneself when faced by the opposition of someone else's way of thought. And human progress takes place only because of these obstacles and of the effort required for surmounting them. But not all disagreements are fruitful. Between Nazism and Communism or between Nazism and Christianity (and the Western way of thinking which stems from it) there was not, and there never will be, any possible dialogue: there is only steel and fire, because Nazism is fundamentally *inhuman*, because its basic conception of what is human is irreconcilable with Christianity as with Communism. Whereas these two ways of looking at the human race are, on the contrary, only two methods of thinking which diverge from a common basic idea. And so the confrontation of one with the other may be a source of fresh light. However, I repeat, this confrontation would have to take place with this basic agreement as its starting point, for if one tried to ignore it and to begin a dialogue directly on the points of disagreement, the only result would be to accentuate them still more, and so to increase one's isolation – to accentuate precisely the gap one is trying to reduce. This is what I have been trying to make people understand in my recent works. It is what I meant when I said, earlier on, that I write in order to 'try to help my readers to find the meaning of their life'. I meant that, in order to approach a dialogue fruitfully, each of the antagonists must first make the effort to set aside for a moment his system of beliefs, the effort to look for what there is in common between his adversary and him. Well, what both of them have in common is that they are men. It is, therefore, upon an idea of man, and of the meaning of the human, that they must reach agreement before pushing the discussion further, and it is to that agreement that, as a man of peace, I dedicate my pen and my efforts.

THE PROBLEMS OF FRENCH WRITERS (1955)

In the course of a conversation with a Soviet writer, the talk turned on *The Mandarins* by Simone de Beauvoir.

'Can you explain to me,' your writer asked, 'why French literature has become mainly a literature of ideas? In the work of your best novelists the characters no longer have independent life. They express the novelist's ideas. Is this not true of Sartre, of Camus in *The Pest*, and of yourself in your *Borderline*?'

'That is perhaps a little sweeping,' I replied. 'To begin with, my case is a special one. Am I a *real* novelist? I don't think so. Any more than I used to be a *real* painter. I don't much care for these schoolroom classifications. I try to be a human being, and that is quite difficult enough. Formerly I drew and now I try to write exactly what I have to say, without worrying about whether, in doing so, I fall into this or that category or not. But, I am well aware, I do not represent French literature!'

'All the same,' said the writer, 'isn't that true also of most of you?'

'Most of us? I don't know. It holds good for Sartre and for Camus. For Malraux, too, to a large extent. For a good many others, too – you are right. But all the same. . . . There are still quite a lot of thoroughbred novelists, who put the truth of their characters before their own ideas.'

'Not many,' said the writer, 'and not the most interesting ones. It was recognized, indeed, quite recently by one of your writers, Maurice Blanchot – although he himself could not manage, in spite of the advice he gave, to avoid the literature of ideas. That is just what is surprising. I should like to understand what has happened.'

'No doubt,' I said, 'it is because a "real" novelist has no further function within French society in the state it is in. To depict characters? But which ones? And above all, depict them for whom? Don't forget that, for the most part, the French writer has come from the *bourgeoisie*. He has drunk its milk, he speaks its language, and his way of thinking was shaped in it. That is true even of many Communist writers, who write against the *bourgeoisie*, but in language and in ways of thinking which can only be understood by *bourgeois* readers. *Bourgeois* thinking in France, and therefore necessarily that of French writers, has been worked through and through by a series of intellectual acrobatics which are, as it were, signs by which they know one another, old school ties. I remember one evening at dinner sitting next to a doctor who told me that one ought to learn Latin, because it was a means of recognizing one's own kind later in life. *Bourgeois* thinking is aristocratic, and few writers who have fed on it too thoroughly are able to escape from it.

'It follows that, with a few exceptions, the only public for a French writer, even an anti-*bourgeois* one, is still an essentially *bourgeois* public. Not to mention the price of books, which puts them outside the range of the popular public. There are indeed some cheap series, whose merely middling success (when compared with the sales of books in the Soviet Union and even in America) shows that the real reason lies elsewhere. The real reason is that the French writer still does not know how to write for the people, and the people cold-shoulders him – is not keen even on the progressive writers, because they too are not easy for it to follow.

'In the case of the conservative or reactionary writers this *bourgeois* public is one they have always had and they desire no other. And it is therefore among them that there are still to be found the majority of the "real" novelists that remain. Yet you are right in saying that they are getting fewer. I will tell you why. I am, of course, oversimplifying, but the reason is that most of them too have lost faith. They no longer believe in their heart of hearts, as they used to do, in the *bourgeoisie* for which they continue to write. If you write for the *bourgeoisie*, what does it want you to tell it? *Bourgeois* stories. But what stories? In their time, Barrès, Bourget and even Proust could still depict the *bourgeoisie* as it was, before the 1914 war, with its weaknesses and vices. Because it still had virtues. And because these virtues could justify its being the ruling class of a great and prosperous country. But today, in the spasms of its decline, these virtues are stifled by the instinct of self-preservation. And to depict the weaknesses and vices of a class when it is losing its virtues and when death threatens it, would be to betray it. Therefore a *bourgeois* writer, and one still proud of being so, can no longer depict his own class as he sees it. All honour to Mauriac for doing so all the same. He is the only one, or almost. The others have not his courage. Cannot they, you will say, depict virtuous *bourgeois*, in order to set them up as an example? But ever since André Gide there has been a dogma, which no *bourgeois* novelist would dare to transgress: that fine sentiments make poor literature. They would die of shame if they were accused by the critics of "edifying literature". So here they are, caught between two fires. Either to be traitors or to be ridiculous. They get out of it by no longer depicting characters. They agitate ideas.

'But, you may say, for the progressive writer these obstacles do not exist, do they? That is true, they do not. Then what holds him back? The fact that he is in a still more uncomfortable position. Because it is no longer enough for him to write for a *bourgeoisie* which is, none the less, the only, or almost the only, class that reads him: that is the contradiction in which he is placed. He doesn't want to please it. Or to amuse it. He doesn't want to tell a diverting story: that would be one more complicity. To depict the vices of that society? Certainly, and he does so. But this already involves him in producing a literature of ideas, in taking sides, in expressing an opinion. And besides, he is no longer very interested in that. What is required is to precipitate the agony, not to depict its convulsed features.

'What is left to him? To try and find the man under the *bourgeois*. To show the reader precisely how the *bourgeois* in him today betrays the man. To give him in this way a bad conscience. To weaken his already decidedly tottering faith in his class supremacy. All of which things belong essentially to the literature of ideas.

'But, you will say, why the devil persist in depicting either *bourgeois* or nothing? Why not depict the people?

'There are several reasons. . . . The one I have already given – that *bourgeois* readers want to read stories about *bourgeois* is obviously not decisive. (It counts, all the same.) The chief one is that, to depict the people, you must first know the people. You need to have lived with it all through its labours, sorrows and joys.

'Well, not only are there still few writers in France who have really come from the people, but in addition, very often, the *bourgeoisie* has got hold of them. Compared with one Stil or one Laffite, who have remained faithful to their popular origin even in their manner of writing, what a lot of Guéhennos there are –

what a lot of Louis Guilloux (first writing *La Maison du Peuple*, then gradually composing his *Jeu de Patience*, brimful of poetry and talent, but amounting to nothing but an interminable old school tie for the enlightened reader only!). This is not a reproach. Just as thought cannot gain in refinement and ease without becoming sophisticated, so a writer could not simplify his thought without denaturing it. It is difficult, if not impossible, to sort out the true from the false treasures accumulated during a lifetime, for they are too closely bound up together, and in trying to get rid of the false ones there is a great danger of the true ones being sacrificed at the same time. But if those writers who were born among the people have lost the power of speaking to it, how should those who were not so born gain it? Hardly any of us comes from the proletariat, and while Aragon in his *Communistes*, and Vailland in his *Beau Masque*, have succeeded in the *tour de force* of escaping from that terrible "populism" which "studies the working-class man", and in depicting workers plausibly in spite of their *bourgeois* origin, it is still none the less a *tour de force*, and you cannot make a whole literature out of *tours de force*.

'We have other troubles. They are much more complex than in your country. The relations between content and form, in the Soviet Union, raise the same problems for all your writers. This is not yet the case in France.

'Formerly, the conservative or reactionary spirit expressed itself in the form as much as in the content. There are no writers more classic in their technique than Maurras or Barrès. This is why, in the revolt against his own class, the writer began by attacking academicism, and in fact, from Rimbaud to Surréalisme, the *bourgeoisie* recognized in these destroyers its most dangerous enemies, and it pursued them with its hatred and its sarcasms. But now, with events, things have changed. The revolutionary spirit now tends to express itself directly, because riddles, however violent, are no longer seemly in face of Oradour, Auschwitz and Hiroshima. And meanwhile the intellectual *bourgeoisie* had also come to understand (more or less consciously) that there was no better strategy for blunting revolt than that of mingling with the rebels. It must be said also, in all honesty, that it has always had a bad conscience, and that its better part constantly tends to join its own detractors, to admire them and therefore to imitate them. In its form, all the reactionary writing of these last thirty years has aped that of its adversaries, and so has drowned in apparent revolt the cry of the genuine men of the revolt. This was all the more deceptive since the movement of revolutionary minds in the opposite direction did not take place immediately, and during the whole period between the two wars it was very hard to distinguish the one side from the other. Besides, many of these sham revolutionaries were caught by their own game, and sincerely believed themselves to be true ones. Even now it is often difficult to distinguish them, even though, paradoxically, it is now *bourgeois* writing that, as a whole, has taken on the revolutionary form, and revolutionary writing that has assumed the traditional form. For there are still many progressive minds who retain, in spite of themselves, an obscure prejudice against the classic forms of expression; who fear that, in going back to them they may be taking a retrograde step, making a concession to academicism, or even supporting the *bourgeois* reaction. The reaction, of course, carefully fosters this confusion, for this fear on the part of progressive minds is not entirely unfounded. And so the *bourgeoisie* wins both ways.

'This would be enough – even if there had not also been, in the present social condition of France, other and even stronger reasons – to make the progressive writers, in this difficult debate, look for a point of support in criteria external to literature. Some of them have found it in Marxism, and for them the problem is solved. But most of the others – like Sartre, like myself – cannot fully subscribe to it. It would take too long to explain the reason here. There remains a considerable part of our questionings – the death of dear ones, the suffering of a child, the insurmountable obstacle presented by nature to all real knowledge – to which Marxism provides no answer of a kind that will quiet them. Such people seek their light in what precedes Marxism, if I may say so, as also in what precedes literature: they seek it in the fundamental significance of the *human*.

'To be frank, they have been led to this search not only by what is happening in their own country, in France, but also, to a large extent, because of what they see happening in yours. They have certainly the most lively admiration for Soviet literature: Sholokhov, and Fedin (together with many others) are wondrous names to them. And they often find much to learn from this literature. And yet, to satisfy them altogether, it lacks something essential. This is difficult to explain in one word, but if I must, I should say that the something might be called disquiet.

'Self-criticism is not the same thing as disquiet. The criticism of institutions is not, nor is that of the men in power, nor is that of the working of the social machinery. Disquiet is a disposition of the mind to be never satisfied. In the scientist it is the tyrannical impulse always to go on inquiring; it is to find, if need be, the courage to cast doubt on everything once more, even when he thinks he has got hold of the truth. In the artist, in the writer, it means never being content with a fixed image of what man is or ought to be, and of what he is doing on this planet.

'I remember another conversation, during my first visit to Moscow, with some Soviet writers. It was about just this particular concern of mine to inquire ever more deeply into what is the essence of the *human*. "That seems to us useless, and no doubt dangerous too, in so far as such a search disconcerts the reader," they said. "We find the real essence of the human in the great examples: we find it in the young heroes of Krasnodar, we find it in Meresseyev, or in Fucik, or in your Péri and your Jean Prévost. Those are the men who really define the human figure in its highest acceptance. That is enough for us. We feel no need to go and compare ourselves with the ape."

'At that moment – it was before the explosion of a certain affair in the U.S.S.R., which showed that it is possible even in your country, to confuse a criminal with a hero for a long time, and for a hero to become a criminal – I contented myself with replying that the figure of a hero was a less simple thing in our country. Because, with us, one of the heroes of the 1914 war became, under the Occupation, the head of one of the wickedest Fascist militias in the world. Because one of the heroes of the

French Resistance has become, since then, the bloody repressor of popular resistance in the French Union. Rommel and Balbo were heroes to their own countries: should they be taken as examples? And what about the Nazis who died standing their ground at Stalingrad? 'This is what compels progressive writers, in France as in the rest of the West, never to be at rest. They know that the noblest of men and the noblest of causes are always in danger of one day going wrong, through according too rigid a faith to their certainties. That hero of the First World War had more faith in order and the hierarchy than in his country: he betrayed France and his people. That resister had more faith in his country and Christianity than in the human species: he betrayed Christian charity and the honour of France. It is not for me to say what has happened in the case of Beria, or in the case of the judges who in Hungary condemned men who have, since then, had to be rehabilitated: most certainly they let their faith stray to some false idea. This is what keeps the progressive French writer in the state of what I have just called "disquiet" – non-quietude. This it is that forces him to seek, as I do, always and ceaselessly, over and above what he believes to be true *at the given moment*, something truer still, immutably true and forming that essence of the *human* which a man cannot betray without betraying everything.

'That,' I said, in conclusion, to my friend the Soviet writer, 'that is why, of course along with countless other reasons, the progressive writer in France is not always one of those thorough-bred novelists who put the truth of their characters before the truth of their ideas. But am I to admit that, as you think, he is abandoning to some extent, by so doing, the great tradition of the French novel? You see, I am not at all sure. You refer to Stendhal, Balzac, Proust and Roger Martin du Gard. But, parallel to that tradition, there is another which has never ceased to exist: that of the fighting novelists, if I may put it so – that of Rousseau, Voltaire, the Hugo of *Quartre-vingt-treize*, Vallès and Anatole France. Candide and Jérôme Coignard did not attain their immortality through their truth as living characters: their immortality is that of Voltaire, and that of France, expressing themselves openly through their mouths. After all, they too are references of which we still have the right to be proud.'

.   .   .   .   .

As I have said already, this article did not appear. I had sent it in at the beginning of September 1955. I received a letter asking my permission to cut out the name of Beria. I telegraphed this permission, but accompanied it with the following letter:

10 September 1955

Monsieur T——,
'*Foreign Literature*',
Moscow.

I have naturally read your letter with close attention, and that I might make quite plain the thoughts it has suggested to me I telegraphed to you my agreement to your request: the permission to cut out from my article the name of Beria.

I let you know of this consent straight away, in order that you might not suppose that the aim of the following considerations is limited to a defence of my own text, or some stupid form of author's susceptibility; in order, on the contrary, that it should be firmly established that they go far beyond my own personal case.

I have thought a great deal about your letter, I have weighed every word of it, just as later I weighed every word of the passage which makes you fear 'that it may shock the aesthetic or political feelings of the Soviet reader', and my conclusions are rather grave ones.

For when I alluded to Beria (not 'in passing' nor on the plane of 'aesthetic' issues, but on moral issues that are vital to us writers) I did so for the same *essential* reasons that lead me to refer to two Frenchmen who have betrayed France (as I might also have mentioned Pétain). If, then, I am shocking the feelings of the Soviet reader, I am likewise shocking those of the French reader. I have been shocking these for fifteen years without stopping. My short novel, *The Guiding Star*, published clandestinely, is many times more shocking. For a quarter of a century Pétain was to the French 'the Victor of Verdun', a national hero, and he has even remained so for many people who, even now, cannot believe that a national hero could have become a traitor. Pétain's criminal errors have been an extremely painful matter for all Frenchmen, and still are; but if we felt that people dared not mention them in front of us, that is when we should be shocked and insulted – it would imply that we were considered to be more or less his accomplices.

And so your letter makes me much less optimistic than I thought I was justified in being when I was in your country and you asked me: 'Would writers like Mauriac or Hemingway agree to write for us?' It is true that I myself advised you: 'Make it clear to them at once that of course any reflections that would outrage the feelings of Soviet readers could not be published,' but it never entered my head then that the mere reference to an affair and to a man whose name is no more painful to you than that of Pétain to us – a man who, besides, has filled the columns of *Pravda*, whose culpability was proclaimed to all the world by M. Kruschev at the time of his visit to Tito, and who has provided Korneichuk with the theme of a successful play – could in your view, because it is made by a foreigner, possess this shocking quality. This is no longer a matter of discretion towards the readers' feelings, it is, I am afraid, a taboo. All discussion between Soviet writers and ourselves will be very difficult, and probably sterile, if we know in advance that there will be taboos. I repeat: my article is not in question – the point I was making can, if need be, do without that reference to a Soviet criminal and confine itself (in spite of the injustice of such unilateral reference) to the criminals of my own country. By doing so it loses, however, the quality of *universality* which was fundamental to my mind. So my truncated esposition is no longer absolutely honest, for it will seem to admit implicitly that such errors naturally cannot occur under a Soviet régime. Yet if I thought they could not occur there, there would be no longer any problem, for I should have become a Communist years ago – and so, probably, would S—— and many o hers. I did not become one because, in the meantime, there occurred the Budapest trials, and I was not allowed to make plain my uneasiness about them in the Communist Press, and this

E

interdiction showed me that on this capital point there was still too great a divergence of ethics between us. I have told you that, this time, I had great confidence in the possibility of a real dialogue, because I thought I had understood that in your review our divergences could be expressed openly, provided of course that they were couched in a friendly and comprehensive form. I repeat once more that I and several others still offer you our collaboration, with or without taboos, because our friendship for the Soviet Union makes us anxious to overcome these dissensions. But I am very much afraid you may not be able to go very far to the right of us. At the first taboo you will see men like Mauriac or Hemingway dart away like a flight of sparrows.

I was determined, my dear friend, to write all this to you with the greatest frankness, because I had based great hopes on the success of your review in starting a fruitful dialogue between the writers and readers of our respective countries, and of differing opinions. It would be a tremendous pity if it should fail. Yet there is danger of this, I am afraid. Perhaps it will seem to you and your friends worth further weighing and discussion.

I hope so, and again assure you very sincerely of all my wishes for success, and of my friendship.

V.

Five months went by before I received a reply to this letter. It came at last: they would not publish the article, in spite of my permission to cut out the name of Beria; because they neither wished to leave it in, nor to remove it when I was so obviously not in agreement. Besides, many other points were controversial, it would have been necessary to start a discussion in the columns of the review, and that did not seem desirable for a start. They said they were very sorry and assured me once more of their high consideration and great friendship. In my turn I replied, in the following letter:

20 February 1956

Monsieur T——,
'*Foreign Literatu e*',
Moscow.

I certainly bear you no ill will for the time you took in answering me, and on the contrary I am grateful to you for the care you have taken in doing so and the frank explanation you give me.

At first sight, one might fear that this has been a bad beginning of contact, but if one looks closer, it is far from being as bad as that.

In all human relations people constantly have the illusion that these are simple and can go fast. And then it becomes clear that there are still plenty of obstacles. The danger then, obviously, is to get discouraged. This would be the last thing to do. For as long as the obstacles remain vague and hidden in the mist, one does not know how to cope with them. But when they are out in the broad daylight one can size them up and think how to reduce them.

When you asked me for that article – and confided to me your hope that fruitful discussions between foreign non-Communist writers and Soviet writers might be established through your review – you had not fully sized up the obstacles. Neither had I, when I agreed to write the article, and when I wrote it as I did, sized up the obstacles to its publication. Here we are now, on both sides, with these obstacles plain and visible before us, and we have already avoided one of them – an enormous one: that of sheering off and turning our backs on one another, telling ourselves that all these mountains are decidedly too high to be crossed.

Naturally I cannot help regretting that my article did not appear! That is very natural for a man of letters, and besides, it would have been a joy and an honour for me to be the French writer to have started the great confrontation with our Soviet colleagues. I am sad at giving this up: but luckily I am past the age of childish disappointments, and this negative side of our adventure weighs on my spirit only slightly. What I regret more seriously is that my article could not be of use as I hoped, precisely in stimulating the Soviet writers to reply to me, and to refute me or even counter-attack me, on the point which I raised (the *quality* of disquiet in Soviet writers), for this is precisely one of the points which anti-Communist propaganda in France (and in the West in general) emphasizes in intellectual circles, and on which we – the non-Communist writers – would like to see more light thrown, that we might understand better.

You yourself tell me that I wrote my article in the heart of my own country, where what I say appears to my French readers in a light they are used to, but would be much more difficult for Soviet readers to grasp in its true light. Well, naturally this applies also to our country, as regards the way in which things happen in Soviet literary circles; I mean that, with us, the difficulty is reciprocal, and that what seems immediately understandable within the Soviet Union is not so to the same extent in Paris or London.

For this reason I had high hopes of the discussions which could not have failed to follow the publication of my article. I understand – though without grasping the deeper reasons – that it is not considered desirable, at least at present, to open these discussions on the public platform formed by your review. And this although I should myself have been led at once to define certain ideas which, your letter shows me, I have not explained clearly enough – for instance that idea of disquiet, which you interpret as a determination to refuse on principle any unshakable conviction: yet nothing is further from my thought! I am the first to have unshakable convictions, about which I feel not the slightest 'disquiet'! What I meant is that we hold that there must always remain a *creative* disquiet, which applies to the future, never to what is past and done with, and which may throw doubt on this or that method used to make these unshakable convictions prevail, but never on the existence of these convictions themselves. In the example I took, absence of doubt would have consisted in saying: 'They are arresting fourteen doctors. They must be right,' and doubt in saying: 'Are they sure they do well to arrest these doctors? Have all precautions been taken to guarantee a scrupulous application of Soviet justice?' But in no case to say to oneself: 'Are Soviet justice and the Soviet régime good?' It is in the West, in anti-Communist circles, that people gladly slide from one proposition to the other and try to involve the progressive writers in this confusion. And it is precisely by clearly demonstrating our uneasiness about this or that method of government or administration which threatens to go contrary to the deep set laws of democracy and to *retard their progress*, that we defend our unconditional attachment to our democratic convictions. That was my point, and it is one on which many people in France would be happy to hear or to read the opinion of Soviet writers. But if it is too early for such a discussion to take place publicly in a review, is it impossible to imagine its being conducted in, for the moment, a more discreet fashion? For example, could not what I wrote be submitted to a few Soviet writers, in order that they might reply to me? Would not this be a first step in the direction of a more and more open debate, which we might even hope to take up again later, in order to make it public in the acceptable form which might perhaps, after some time, emerge from these personal and discreet discussions? The idea might also be considered of bringing this sort of private dialogue to the knowledge of a few chosen writers in France, in order to get from them, in their turn, their reaction, without making any public use of it. Would not this be a way of planting a young tree – a tree of understanding – which might later begin to grow and blossom? I make this suggestion *en toute simplicité*: you may find obstacles to its favourable reception, of which I have not thought (but to know them, too, would again help me where I am ignorant). In any case, this will have shown you how far I am from taking offence at the decision to reject my article, and how anxious I am, on the contrary, to derive from it, if possible, the benefit which lies at the bottom of every difficulty, even if at first it seems discouraging.

This letter received no answer. In the meantime (in the preceding November) the French review, France-U.R.S.S., *had asked me for an article in favour of peaceful relations between the two countries. I suggested a more substantial and useful subject: the conditions necessary in my view for the establishing of a fruitful dialogue between French and Soviet writers. The review agreed to this. A few days later, therefore, I sent in the following article:*

THE CONDITIONS FOR THE DIALOGUE (1955)

Those who, like me, have concentrated their efforts on pre-venting the cold war from leading in the long run to a final divorce between two worlds, two cultures, two philosophies, have had many reasons for rejoicing since the coming of the period of 'détente'. It really is – to use the title of Ehrenburg's novel – *The Thaw*. No doubt it began rather badly (this is not surprising), and many of us will not quickly forget the appalling incident of the Soviet Ballet, prevented from dancing by a government composed of miserable idiots, which wanted to get its own back for a military defeat. The Moïsseiev Ballets have, since then, magnificently effaced this bitter piece of tomfoolery, after the Peking Opera had melted the last snows. The roads are now clear. The caravans can set out to begin their valuable exchanges.

The conditions for these exchanges are beginning to grow plain. They now involve more than initiative by individuals, or even by groups, if it is desired that these exchanges should turn out to be really fruitful. For what is required is no longer to secure some hole and corner conversation with some isolated Soviet writer who has been made to wait three months for a three day visa. It is that all Soviet writers should be able to come to France with the same freedom as the Italian or Swedish writers (not to mention the American writers, who can come to our country as they wish, while for us to go to them requires a most improbable visa) – on a basis of reciprocity, of course. This, therefore, depends on the governments. It is not an impossible thing: it appears that the government of a neighbouring country, more intelligent than ours, has taken the first step, and that a meeting between eminent Western and Soviet writers is to take place there very soon. Once again we shall have missed the bus, leaving to others the advantage of leading the way. The aim of this meeting, if it takes place, is a beginning and, perhaps, to prepare the way for a larger congress: will Paris let this too escape it, when the time comes?

But let us suppose the problem solved. Let us suppose that these meetings do take place, and that at the same time our reviews open their pages to the Soviet writers, and the Soviet reviews open theirs to our writers. Will the conditions for an exchange then be fulfilled?

These things are certainly necessary, but they are far from

being sufficient. The main obstacles will come from the writers themselves, and from the prejudices which ten years of complete rupture have firmly rooted on both sides.

On the Western side, unquestionably, the main obstacle will come from a certain unwillingness to believe that the dialogue is possible. People have not forgotten the outrageous scandal at the last congress of the P.E.N. Club, when its president declared in his speech that the P.E.N. could never consent to hobnob with writers 'who denounce their own colleagues'. He did indeed try, a little later, to pretend he had not meant what he had said, but this piece of clumsiness, if it was one, is symptomatic of a long-standing state of mind. Even while I am writing, a debate is going on in Paris on the subject: 'The chances of a dialogue with Soviet intellectuals' – with this peculiarity, that those who have been put down to speak have all, as though by chance, proclaimed more than once that such chances do not exist. None of the non-Communist writers who have already started the dialogue has (or so it seems) been invited to give an account of his opinion or his experience. And I can guess, in advance, the resolution that will be adopted at the conclusion of this exemplary meeting: the dialogue will only be possible, it will be said, when the Soviet writers consent to controvert their own institutions.

Well, anyone who has talked with them, as I have, in private and in public, knows perfectly well that they are the first to criticize with the greatest freedom many practices, routines and errors of their administration. But he knows also that none of them would for a single second contemplate calling the régime itself into question. The Soviet writer's trust in Socialism is as strong as the faith of a Christian writer in the existence of God. To subject the chances of a dialogue to the condition that one or other of them should first go back publicly on this conviction amounts to refusing the dialogue hypocritically while putting the blame for the refusal on the other side.

Those Western writers who are sincerely desirous of participating in the 'thaw' of our two cultures will have, therefore, to reject this deliberate mystification and to admit within themselves, first of all, that Communism is not (as a certain Papal

Bull would have it) 'intrinsically perverse', any more than are those writers who have freely decided to write within the Communist perspective.

On the Soviet side the obstacles are more or less the corresponding ones. But they are well on the way to disappearing. Only a slight effort would be needed for them to be flattened out completely.

A few years ago the Soviet Union was still in the situation of a besieged city: America's military bases and superiority in nuclear weapons forced the U.S.S.R. to maintain in all fields an iron cohesion, in order not to succumb. At that time anyone who went about outside the walls repeating that all was not always well inside the city, could only be taken for an enemy of its citizens, even if he declared himself a friend. But things have changed. The nuclear lag has been abolished, and the Soviet Union no longer has need, for self-preservation, of this siege psychology. In consequence it willingly accepts free criticism. Accepts? Desires it. The following story will serve as proof (I hope its heroes will not blame me for indiscretion in reporting here a private conversation). It happened this summer near Moscow in Surkov's *datcha*. The great novelist, Leonid Leonov was there, among other friends. Conversation was lively. Suddenly, turning to me, Leonov said: 'What do you think of S——? He is rather a mystery to us. Is he really honest?' Naturally, though rather surprised, I thought there must be still some lingering mistrust of S—— on account of his earlier writings. I replied that, as far as I knew, S—— was unquestionably one of the French writers who spoke his own mind most honestly. 'There is, all the same,' said Leonov, 'something we don't understand. Look: he came here last year. We took him everywhere, he saw everything he wanted to see. Absolutely everything. We hid nothing from him.' (I was naturally beginning to be worried. What could S—— have done?) 'When he got back to France,' Leonov went on, 'he wrote a whole series of articles. You read them. . . .' (Not all. I grew more and more worried. Had he made some *faux pas*?) 'Well, you see,' Leonov concluded, 'he found *everything* all right. Everything. Not a single criticism. After all, not everything in our country is as

perfect as all that; there are improvements to make, and defects
to put right. S—— must have known this – we told him; and
yet he doesn't breathe a word of it in his articles. That is why
I ask you, is he really honest?'

You can imagine my amusement at this unexpected conclusion. And at being obliged to defend S—— by explaining
why people like him (or like me), that is to say, people who are
reputed to be friends of the Soviet Union, are often, in fact,
forced to keep certain minor criticisms to themselves, because
these would be immediately blown up, exaggerated and
cynically exploited against their friends by an unscrupulous
Press. We have to save up our freedom to criticize for the really
important or really grave cases, like, for instance, the Rajk
affair, which for a long time set me at loggerheads with the
French Communists. This explanation reassured Leonov, who
expressed delight at hearing that a man can be honest even
without criticizing the U.S.S.R. . . . .

The tone, it will be admitted, is a somewhat new one. And
it seems that henceforward there should be no further difficulties, from the Soviet side, in the way of a dialogue. This is not
yet quite certain. I will explain why.

A few days earlier I had spent the afternoon in another
datcha, belonging to the editor of the new review, *Foreign
Literature*. He had asked me my opinion about many things,
among them this: did I think that writers whose sympathy for
the Soviet Union is only slight, like Camus or Hemingway,
would answer, if the review were to ask them their opinion – expressed with complete freedom – on a given question? I replied
that, with some of them, the danger would rather be that they
might answer, but in such terms that the review would be
unable to publish their answer, and that they would take
advantage of this to say, triumphantly: 'Here you have proof
that there can be no dealings with those people!' They would,
therefore, I suggested, have to be frankly warned that the
review, however desirous it might be of publishing the most
divergent opinions, would naturally do so only if these were
expressed in fair terms, such as to take into consideration the
feelings of Soviet readers. 'I think,' I added, 'that many of

them will answer even so, and those who do not answer will thus be implicitly confessing that they would only have done so to injure you.'

Back in France, I wrote the article which I myself was asked to contribute on 'The Problems of French Writers'. As can be imagined, it was expressed in 'fair terms'. And yet, after sending it, I received a letter asking me to consent to the suppression of a passage 'which would hurt the feelings of the Soviet reader'. The passage in question was a short allusion – alongside Pétain, Darnand and the murderers in Indo-China and elsewhere – to a man who was, to Soviet Russia, the equivalent of what those men were to the France of the Resistance. I replied frankly – and I repeat here – that this request for suppression seemed to me a grave matter. Not as regards the cut itself, which indeed I willingly authorized, considering its slight importance in my text. But because this semi-censorship presupposed that there were subjects forbidden only contributors from abroad – since the columns of *Pravda* had been full of the affair, and one of the best Soviet playwrights had recently taken it as the theme of a successful play.

Certainly, when in our country a foreigner speaks to us of the treason of a former hero of Verdun, this is painful to our national pride. And Soviet susceptibility is similarly understandable. But after all, I asked, if no one is willing to overcome his own susceptibility, what are we going to talk about? If we cannot approach the themes which are, precisely, our mutual subjects of incomprehension or uneasiness, if we can discuss nothing but flowers or butterflies, what sort of dialogue will that be? Does anyone think that such a prospect will attract many of the hesitant? Such were the questions I put. I have still received no reply to my letter, and I do not know what they thought of it all.

But I think we have there one of the points which show, on the Soviet side, that the desire to be subjected to criticism in a friendly way has not yet perhaps been as fully freed from the old prejudices as Leonov liked to think. That prejudice was too old a habit and had too long been necessary for there to be any chance of its disappearing so quickly and leaving no traces.

It is only from a genuine effort on both sides – an effort of tact and understanding on this side, and of tolerance and, I might say, unconstrainedness on the other side – that the possibility of a really sincere and fruitful dialogue will be born – and in consequence, of a far more valuable enrichment of both our cultures.

.   .   .   .   .

This article likewise did not appear. I was asked by telephone to cut out certain things (not only certain passages that might have shocked the Russians, but also the Americans, and even M. Ngo Din Diem . . .). I suggested not cutting them, but changing them. My suggestions seemed to be accepted. But next day I received a letter which insisted afresh on the necessity of cuts rather than changes. I replied:

17 December 1955

Monsieur M. P——,
Review *France-U.R.S.S.*,
Paris.

I had told you, and confirmed in writing, that I could understand *France-U.R.S.S.* considering the publication of an article like mine premature. I had told you also that I could see no point in writing the sort of anodyne article for which you asked me: what is the good of my coming out in favour of relations which everyone (except the warmongers) wants as we do, unless it is to define the conditions which seem to me indispensable in order to turn a pious hope into an effective reality?

But today you give me to understand that my article is not only considered premature but fundamentally incompatible with the Review's rule of never intervening in the questions which I raise.

As these questions are precisely those which, in my view, have to do with the elementary duties of writers, and as I personally cannot envisage any fruitful dialogue on other bases, all that remains for me to do is to ask you to return my article.

I am sorry that these problems, which I have discussed openly in the U.S.S.R. with several Soviet writers, cannot be mentioned in your columns. This, as I have already said to you, will greatly limit the desired widening of relations. I still think it is a great pity.

The review replied that there had evidently been a misunderstanding at the start: for, since its aim was a rapprochement, *the review could not publish attacks that might estrange, even in France, people whom it was desired to win over. I replied again:*

27 December 1955

Monsieur P——,
Review *France-U.R.S.S.*,
Paris.

There may indeed have been a misunderstanding, though not as great a one as you suppose. The conditions I consider necessary for a dialogue do not apply only to the Soviet reviews, they apply first to ours. If all one can write in them is what will not shock any reader or contain any risk of estranging him, it is hardly worth while to write in them: that is what I call one of the first duties of the writer.

The sentences you are asking me to suppress are not very important in themselves, they are important in so far as, by consenting to suppress them, I should myself be going against my deep-seated intentions.

Besides, these cuts would be illogical if they were not completed by others: how should one leave in 'a government of miserable clowns' if one suppresses the 'murderers in Indo-China', since these are the same people? Why allow me to accuse the P.E.N. Club, of which many of your readers are members? Or the 'intellectuals' who have met without us, since they, according to you, are to be won over (and anyhow this passage has now lost all topicality)? And why, finally, leave in the allusion to Beria, even though he is not named, if the allusion to Rajk, even though he is not named, is forbidden?

I do not think that, to achieve the dialogue, we should start by hiding our personal position, but on the contrary should first proclaim it in order, afterwards, to be able to confront it with the people who think differently. That is what is meant by dialogue. Between Frenchmen, just as much as with the Russians.

That is how I personally have long carried it on, with both these. Why should I go back to a less advanced position? It would be contrary to everything I am trying to do.

I am saying all this, not in order to persuade the Review to revoke its decision and to urge it to publish my text as it is – quite the contrary: it is in fact now too late for that particular text. There have been new facts meanwhile, I have received certain explanations, and it would no longer be opportune to publish my difference with *Foreign Literature* – there would be danger of seeming anxious to envenom it.

I should therefore be grateful if you would in any case send back my text, which is now unusable.

Rest assured that I have no hard feelings as the result of this *contretemps*, except regret for a missed opportunity.

Another time!

When I wrote 'another time', to Frenchmen just as to the Russians, I really thought I was noting a provisional failure due solely to an error in my own appreciation of the opportunity, which I had been anxious not to let slip, of precipitating a development that seemed to me already far advanced.

Was I wrong? I am far from believing so, even today. All this occurred several months before the Twentieth Congress. I had certainly been too far ahead, but would I not soon meet, at last, with the understanding which had been lacking? A year later (in the summer of 1956) there were many signs that enabled me to hope so. Poland, where the rumblings prophetic of the 'October revolution' were to be heard, asked me to take charge of a special number about France;[1] and the U.S.S.R. entrusted me with organizing an exhibition of reproductions of French painting: both of them in a spirit of wide curiosity and, for the first time, boldness, which augured well for the future.

The Hungarian tragedy threw everything once more into question.

. . . . .

On the evening that followed the second Soviet intervention, when the

[1] This special number of the review *Tworczosc* (Creation) did in fact appear in April 1957.

*French radio was giving its fullest coverage to an over-zealous protest by
a group of longstanding enemies of Communism, to whom other men
carried away by their disappointment and bitterness were already rallying,
I tried to escape from being swept off my feet by a painful indignation
whose danger was clear to me.*

*That night I wrote a protest which, it seemed to me, should be
capable of uniting those whose consciences had rebelled, without turning
our disgust into an asset to Western imperialism and its hypocritical
expressions of condemnation.*

*When morning came, I telephoned it to Louis de Villefosse, that he
might put it up to his friends. It appeared next day in the Press, signed
by J.-P. Sartre, Claude Roy, Roger Vailland, Claude Morgan, Simone
de Beauvoir, J.-F. Rolland, Louis de Villefosse, Janine Bouissounouse,
and, after a few minor changes, by Michel Leiris, Jacques Prévert,
Colette Audry, Jean Aurenche, Pierre Bost, and several others:*

The undersigned writers have given sufficient evidence of
their friendship for the U.S.S.R. and their loyalty to Socialism[1]
to have the right, today, to protest to the Soviet Government
against the use of guns and tanks to break the revolt of the
Hungarian people and its will to independence, even if the
Fascist elements whose appeals have been heard on the radio
of the insurgents joined in this revolt.

We think and will always think that Socialism cannot, any
more than liberty, be brought on the point of bayonets, and
we fear that a government imposed by force may rapidly be
obliged, in order to maintain itself, to use coercion in its turn,
with all its train of injustices, against its own people.

We are especially anxious as to the fate in store for our
colleagues the Hungarian writers, and we take our stand now
in advance against any attack on their lives or liberty.

Having made this clear, we take our stand no less strongly
against the hypocrites who dare to express indignation today
against what they accepted yesterday without turning a hair.
We deny the right of protest against Soviet interference in
Hungary to those who kept silence (when they did not applaud)

---

[1] Subsequently changed to 'having never expressed feelings inimical either to
the U.S.S.R. or to Socialism, consider they have today the right,' etc.

when the United States stifled in bloodshed the liberty won by
Guatemala. We deny this right to all those who dare to speak
of a 'Prague *coup*' at the very instant when they are noisily
applauding the 'Suez *coup*'. We deny this right to a minister who
carries cynicism, at the moment when his parachutists are
invading Egyptian soil, so far as to dare to speak of the liberty
of nations and to abuse in pathetic tones those who dare to
attack it.

The first thing we ask of the Soviet Government, as of the
French Government, can be put in one word: truth. Where it
prevails, crime is impossible; where it goes under, there can be
no justice, peace, or liberty.

*A few days later Jean-Paul Sartre defined his attitude in L'Express
and went a considerable way beyond this declaration which he had joined
in signing. His condemnation was categorical, left no room for excuse and
appeared irrevocable. 'I break,' he said, 'with the Communists. I break
with my friends the Soviet writers, who will not or cannot protest against
the crimes of their government.'*

*As drafter and promoter of the joint declaration, it seemed to me
necessary to define, in my turn, my personal attitude, which differed
largely from that of Jean-Paul Sartre. The first draft was shelved –
I found it too long, too uncertain in its bases, and, finally, too evasive in
its conclusions to serve its purpose. I publish it none the less, because it
gives quite a good picture of the movement of my thought, its torments
and hesitations, at that period, and so throws light on the texts which will
follow it.*

Jean-Paul Sartre has just defined his attitude towards the
Hungarian drama. He and I, together with others, had given,
before this, our signatures to a declaration condemning the
armed intervention of the U.S.S.R. against the insurgents. For
my part, I not only signed this declaration, I am in fact
responsible for it, and it was I who drafted it, and a certain
number of our co-signatories made up their minds to join us
for the same reasons as I, some of these rather different from
those of Jean-Paul Sartre. I think, therefore, I owe it to them
to formulate these reasons in my turn.

Let us begin by stating the fact that one point is common to us all, a point which it is hardly necessary to recall: the intervention of the Soviet guns has revolted us all; just as we were revolted, at the time, by the crushing of liberty in Guatemala; it has revolted us quite as much as that and even more, because the United States, after all, were only acting in virtue of their basic imperialism, while the U.S.S.R. has struck a blow at the trust we put in its own mission.

And yet I cannot feel this indignation with an even mind. That is where I part company from Sartre. There would be, yes, a kind of peace of mind in being able to be unreservedly indignant, to tell oneself that the U.S.S.R. had no justification for committing this unnatural act. But it had one. There lies the paradox and the tragedy.

A Shakespearian tragedy: Banquo's ghost floats over this bloodstained plot. The ghost of Rajk. That eight-year-old crime has forced the successors of the criminals, the very men who were trying to repair the injustice and to destroy its causes – it has forced them to shed a thousand times more blood, and to endanger Socialism a thousand times more, not only in Hungary but the whole of Europe. 'Foul deeds will rise, though all the earth o'erwhelm them, to men's eyes.'

If any positive lesson could be drawn from this pitiless tragedy, it would be the one which, alas, no one has ever been willing to listen to: the blinding evidence that there is only one realistic policy, and that is to repudiate immoral actions; that, in politics as elsewhere, crimes are paid for the more deeply, the longer they remain buried. But – again alas – Macbeth was never able to change his acts in the slightest, once the first of them was committed: they became stronger than him.

And this is where the paradox becomes agonizing: the Hungarian insurrection was born on the day of Rajk's funeral, then spread, hour by hour, beyond the Communists, then beyond the Socialists, then beyond the Liberals, to be finally swamped by those who, on its last day, spoke to the world to remind it that 'Hungary had always been the advanced bastion against Asiatic barbarism and was in 1945 the last fortress against Bolshevism', and who by so doing identified themselves openly with Nazi Hungary and with the 'anti-Bolshevik crusade' of sinister memory. And already, in fact, the St. Bartholomew's massacre of the Communists had begun. Already, too, that of the Jews, of course. And already, once more, the White Terror was preparing. (But why did not Horthy's Terror – let us not forget it – manage, over twenty years, to arouse the slightest revolt on the part of the Hungarian people?) Certain cruel actions were already not in vengeance for Rajk, but for the beaten Fascists; for let no one tell me that burning men alive in petrol is a Socialist custom. Was the U.S.S.R. to look on, without stirring, at the massacre of its friends? Was it to abandon them? I say frankly, as far as I am concerned, I think that if it had abandoned them, the U.S.S.R. would ·have dishonoured itself even more. Intervention had become inevitable. But what grieves us is precisely that it should have become so – that in ten years Socialism should not have been able to win enough love in the hearts of that people to have united it as one man against frenzied reaction, instead of being, as we have seen, to a certain degree its accomplice, or a consenting party.

I know that, by writing the foregoing, I shall bring down on my head the curses of both sides: is it really the moment, one side will say, to accuse the unfortunate Hungarian insurgents? Is it really the moment, the others will say, to accuse your friends, at a time when in France their homes are being set on fire and the police bludgeon them and protect the incendiaries? I shall once more, I fear, be somewhat rudely handled on all sides for insisting on going about with 'my little conscience worn on my sleeve'. As if it were a matter of one's conscience! I don't care two hoots for my small conscience either at this moment, believe me. I assure you it hardly weighs on me at this moment. But are the rest of you altogether happy at finding yourselves under the banner of M. Tixier-Vignancour? Does it not trouble you? Are you sure that to lump together and magnify the Hungarian insurgents, without reserve, is not an over-simplification, terribly hard on the sincere men who were trying to repair certain wrongs and were the first to get killed? Are you sure, Albert Camus, that you have shown the path of that pure and total Justice for which you fight? And if there was in fact one single just man among the men who were burned alive and one single Nazi who sprinkled him with petrol, what colour will your ink be then? Ah, what would then be the right thing to think? And the right thing to do?

It is too early to reply to you. If I replied now, you would not listen to me. Any more than the Communists will listen to me – than they have ever listened to me, unfortunately. Men of my sort are merely bound to find themselves, in the midst of passions, a little more severely alone than before. But if, all the same, you would like me to tell you what I am doing during these black days – well, in all humility, I am weighing things up. Yes, trying to weigh them up. It is what I have done all my life, including the time when I was writing *The Silence of the Sea*, which, when I published it at the midnight of the Occupation, was considered by many as an evil action, because I depicted a German who was not a monster, and French people who felt no hatred. I am weighing up how much each of these contrary or opposed things contains by way not of total Justice, that cold abstraction of Manichean origin, but, more modestly, of truth and deception, equity or injustice, and above all of hope or perversion; and I am trying to make up my mind according to what I find in the two scales, according to the greater weight. Is this a vain occupation? The answer has been given by the ghost of Rajk, and it will long be there, silent and terrible, giving us its answer. But at the same time, beyond its mute answer, its heavy and bloody answer, I find in spite of everything the greatest weight on the same side, always on the same side. And so, in spite of my revolt and my agony, how should I turn my back on those who alone bear the only hope for the future? For if there is another hope, well, show it me. And so I will remain loyal, obstinately loyal, to those whose errors and blindness I join you today in accusing.

.   .   .   .   .

This first draft, as I have said, was shelved, and I allowed myself a few days' more reflection before attacking a second. It was this second

version that I sent to L'Observateur, *which published it on* 22
November.[1]

BETTER THINGS TO DO

It is now time to try and think honestly.

No armed intervention is justified, and we have declared
this plainly. The ruins of Budapest matter as much as those of
Port Said, the dead at Budapest as much as those in Madagas-
car, the tears of Budapest as much as those of Cyprus or Guatemala. The Red Army, when it crushed the Hungarian workers
under the fire power of its tanks, fought for the first time against
the liberation of a people, and in doing so it has lost its innocence
in the eyes of millions of men. The disappointment has caused
violent anger in many of us, and rightly. But this anger, this
disarray, is now in danger of carrying us too far. We can already
see quite a number of loyal friends of the U.S.S.R. throwing the
helve after the hatchet and condemning to eternal obloquy the
first country of Socialism. Cries that we must never again shake
hands with a Communist are to be heard here and there. This
would not be serious, if these symptoms did not threaten to
spread dangerously, even in the working class.

Dangerously, for we have seen on other occasions how great
is the temptation of becoming a Bergery or a Doriot to a dis-
appointed Communist or a progressive. It is therefore necessary
to examine now, and urgently, what our position is with regard
to the Party and to the U.S.S.R.

Let us recognize, to begin with, that we have no right to
behave like a deceived husband. Certainly we had no exact
idea how far the last ten years had led the peoples of Hungary,
or elsewhere, in the direction of revolt. But it is not true to
claim that we knew *nothing*. We supposed that the Hungarian
proletariat was bravely enduring the present in the name of the
future, but we were not ignorant that this present was made up
of a great many constraints. Often indeed we protested, but,
since we judged that on the scales of good and evil, injustice

---

[1] Many repetitions (Banquo's ghost, etc.) will be found in it, and I apologize
for this. But this is a *dossier*, and I have been unwilling to tamper with the documents.

and hope, it was good and hope that prevailed, our loyalty was not impaired.

Is the equilibrium broken? Do we consider that from now on it is evil and injustice that prevail? We have no right to do anything but proceed afresh to the examination of the balance in which crime is set against hope, in the light of the fires of Budapest.

Who are the men we have condemned in this first flush of indignation? The truth is, they are the very men who, before the insurrection, were trying to restore to Communism the liberal countenance which, for the last ten years, we have been assured it would regain one day – and it was, I repeat, this certainty that justified our loyalty through all the storms and reefs. It is when we have nearly reached port that we have been stricken.

In this light, the Hungarian drama has the cruelty and grandeur of a tragedy by Shakespeare. The ghost of Banquo floats over this bloody tale. The ghost of Rajk, of past crimes and errors. For it is Macbeth's successors, those who were trying precisely to repair his crimes, who today are paying their price: the violent actions of Macbeth are leading them on, in spite of themselves, to more violence and more bloodshed. 'Foul deeds will rise, though all the earth o'erwhelm them, to men's eyes.'

We might crow – those of us who have always proclaimed that any policy which snaps its fingers at moral conscience will later find an irrepressible moral demand rising up against it and forming a terribly real political force. But certain indecent crowings prevent us from doing so (also a certain feeling of relief disguised as gloomy repentance, as pretended disillusionment). And the ignoble display of gleeful indignation, crowned with police violence and bonfires, today dictates our line of conduct. For fear of doubt being cast on our own revolt, we have better things to do now than to shout louder than M. Tixier-Vignancour.

We have better things to do than to stand by and watch the whole of Soviet Russia being abused, 'liberals' being drowned in the same sack with the 'toughs', the young Bolsheviks with the bureaucrats, the courageous reformers with the obstinate opportunists, as if in this shipwreck the whole of the world's hope had foundered irrevocably; instead of helping the just to prevail over the violent in this difficult birth of a new Socialism, from Warsaw to Peking, even if, like all birth, it begins in disorder and bloodshed.

We have better things to do than to quarrel openly with the Soviet writers, with the Soviet people, and to abuse them in their misfortune instead of helping them. We have better things to do than to let the lid, which was raised for a moment, close again over their heads, instead of backing them up in their tragically threatened demand for a widening of their culture.

We have better things to do than to cut ourselves off from the French Communists, who are engaged in one of the most dangerous and painful ordeals in their history. In the presence of those harsh reversals which we are witnessing, what we must try to do with all our strength is to support them against the sclerosis of the obstinate, in their own demand for renovation; not to aid their class enemies to stifle them for ever under the lies which they had believed; not to liquidate the sole safeguard of the French working class.

That is why today, eight years after the Rajk affair, I repeat what I said then, that there is a liberty of which nobody can deprive us, not even the Communists who perhaps will reject us once more as they did then; the liberty to fight for them in spite of our revulsion, in spite of all their errors, in spite of Hungary and perhaps of other tragedies to come, as long as we are sure that the supreme aim, which we are all of us pursuing against wind and tide, and blood and tears, remains alive in their heart of hearts.

.   .   .   .   .

This statement of position brought me in, naturally, a large correspondence. I publish here one of my replies, which sums up well enough those I had to make:

26 November 1956

Mme J. G——,

I am not surprised by your letter, nor by other reactions like yours, which my article will certainly provoke.

I took the risk of this, and the moral responsibility, because in my judgement (at present) it was necessary to say what I said.

The well-known hotch-potch is being concocted, in which, along with 'Guyot, Stil and that ilk',[1] to eat up those who for the last six months have been struggling courageously within the Party; and, in the outside world, enormous populations whose fate depends on People's China, therefore also on the U.S.S.R., however the latter may be behaving just now.

It may seem to you desirable to see 'a clean sweep made of all that'. To me, that would be a crime a hundred thousand times more abominable than the tragedy of Budapest.

I do not think your present indignation comes only from that tragedy. I think that that tragedy enables you to demonstrate more violently certain feelings that were already violent before it.

For the last fifteen years, ever since *The Silence of the Sea*, I have done nothing but try to struggle against violent feelings wherever they come from. I know very well that I shall not be listened to in the present atmosphere. But I have never found, in the refusal to listen to me, a justification for keeping silent.

V.

In the very days that followed, all the co-signatories of the protest received a letter, signed by thirty Soviet writers, which had already appeared in the Literaturnaya Gazeta *in Moscow, in reply to our text — which had indeed been honestly published in* extenso *above the letter.*

That was a quite new fact, in itself completely exceptional and of great significance. For the first time the Soviet reader was being informed of criticisms addressed to his government by foreign writers, not through the reply made to these criticisms, but in the very terms and with the very arguments used by those writers.

Naturally the Soviet reply entitled 'Seeing the Whole Truth' was a categorical refutation of these arguments. It reproached us with not having seen the true reality and with having let ourselves be blinded. But the tone of the reproaches – this also a remarkable fact – was courteous, even friendly. We were not hurled with one gesture into the hell of the heretics. There was, in this letter, more regret than violence.

[1] French Communist figures, reputed to be Stalinists.

It would have to be answered, and since I was the man responsible for the first protest, I set to work on a reply. When I had done, I learnt casually that another, of which I had not been told, was already circulating among the other signatories. If I was being kept out of it did this not mean that my position, as I had defined it in L'Observateur, was disapproved of? If this was the case, would not the reply in question be harsher than mine – perhaps a snub, a refusal of any dialogue? I got in touch with a friendly daily paper, and suggested publishing my text as a matter of urgency. This created some agitation on the editorial staff, but it resulted, in the end, in a favourable decision, and my letter appeared on 28 November.

Soviet friends,

All my efforts for many years have had one aim only – to help to remove the obstacles that separate us. For a long time these efforts have come up against a wall, raised up by errors which we mutually recognize to have been committed on both sides. In the last two or three years we had already had some fine successes. The hope of real and fruitful exchanges was within reach, but now it is obscured in the ashes of Budapest.

You know me, Leonid Leonov, and you, Alexander Surkov, and you, my dear Konstantin Fedin; you cannot have doubts of me; you cannot suppose that if I thought the Hungarian insurrection was only an insurrection of Fascists, I should have wished it not to be crushed. You cannot doubt that, whenever Fascism appears, I shall always be with you, side by side. And yet my friends and I have protested. We have heard the sinister echoes of the massacres of Communists, the *autos-da-fé* and the pogroms which you described to us, and, without perhaps believing them to be as widespread as you say, we have by no means ignored them. We have reckoned up the danger with which they have threatened Hungary, and perhaps the world. And even so, we have protested.

It is therefore evident that, since we were looking this truth in the face, we must have believed also in something else, in something terribly grave, which has wounded us precisely because we love the Soviet Union, precisely because nothing hurts more than seeing those we love act like those we are fighting.

It is for me, therefore, to put you a question: does not the
fact that we, your loyal friends, think like this worry you, in
spite of everything? Are you so sure that you possess 'the whole
truth', as you wrote to us? Can the protests of so many of your
friends who, even at the time of the 'inadmissible violations of
Socialist democracy', even at the time when they were already
protesting against tragic errors (and remember how you
received our protests then . . .), showed towards you an unshakable friendship, of which even now you have no doubts, or
you would not have written to us – yes, can our present protests
leave you so untroubled in mind about *your* truth, about what
at present seems to you to be the truth?

That is all I would like to ask you. The value of this or that
statement which the facts appear to contradict, the absence of
this or that reality which you pass over in silence – these things
we will discuss later, when we can speak of them more calmly,
as I still hope we may.

As I am determined to hope, and am sure I have the right
to hope, we may. For your letter would be pointless if it were
not the beginning of the first real dialogue between us, about
the first real problem to be debated by us seriously. Your letter
would be pointless if it did not mean that you too want 'to see
the whole truth'. And if you speak to us as you do, that is
because you in fact believe that you see it whole – in spite of
the Hungarian working class having risen and made common
cause *with*, not against, the Fascists; in spite of the passive
resistance it is putting up against the Kadar Government; in
spite of the strike in all the factories; in spite of the arrest of
Imre Nagy, of Rajk's widow (Rajk's widow!), captured by
trickery as the Algerian leaders were over here, and, as I write,
vanished, perhaps deported; and in spite of the tragic silence of
the Hungarian writers, of whom, after all, no one dares to think
that they have become Fascist, and of whom, none the less –
this I found painful – you say *nothing*.

What are we writers really – when we are not fighting
simply as citizens and soldiers, with weapons in our hands –
what are we if we are not those who refuse to accept without
examination the truths proposed to them? Who pass them again

and again through the sieve of reason? If we are not those who, like Emile Zola, take a stand, if need be, against the official 'truths', when these seem to them doubtful?

This is why I ask you simply: do you really feel no doubt? Really none, in your heart and conscience? Not even a hesitation?

I ask you merely to answer this simple question. It is all I ask you, I ask nothing more. But I do ask you that urgently – you who once confided to me how bitterly you had felt the revelation of the terrible errors of the past. I ask you that with all my strength, for if you do not answer, we shall have to mourn the loss of a great hope.

But you may not wish to express this answer publicly, in order not to give your enemies here the opportunity of brandishing the slightest uncertainty as an accusation against your country. I could understand that; for in the time when mine was in danger, I would not have been willing to make public my torments and doubts (when, for instance, I saw certain *maquis* abandoned by Free France without help and without weapons, to be crushed). In that case, say nothing, but let us meet, as we have already done, and try to find the truth together. Let us meet where we can meet it too.

Let us meet in Budapest.

. . . . .

The letter from the other signatories appeared next day. To my surprise it was, if anything, less severe than my own. It was more precise, it refuted the arguments of our correspondents point by point but, like mine, in cordial terms. What then was I to conclude from the 'ostracism' to which I had been submitted? Was it simple forgetfulness? If not, why, or to whom, was my signature embarrassing? Why did L'Express *omit my name at the bottom of the very protest I had drafted, and on two occasions represent me as a hopeless 'conformist'? Why was I thus, in both camps, 'rebuffed by everyone'? Just bad luck? No, this was not the first time that I was being pushed aside, and it would not be the last. I would have, one day, to draw the practical conclusions from this quarantine.*

. . . . .

But that would be for later. For the moment what mattered above everything else was that the links with our Soviet colleagues should not be broken. Among them, one man seemed to share my feelings, Ilya Ehrenburg. The papers, at that very time, reported the appeal he had just addressed to his colleagues over the Moscow radio: do not, he said, confuse with your adversaries those friends who, during these sombre days, do not think like us. Do not break off relations! It was easy to conclude from that that the Soviet writers also were divided about us as we were about them, some being in favour of a break, others persevering. To give these latter all possible help seemed to me to be a task of great urgency. Besides, Ehrenburg mentioned me by name as an example. It seemed to me expedient to reply to him in my turn, by name, and to publish the reply in the same paper in which, a week earlier, I had replied to his colleagues. It appeared on 6 December:

4 December 1956

Dear Ilya Ehrenburg,

Have you noticed how often it is at the blackest moment of a storm that the first gleams of fine weather appear? The links between French and Soviet writers have just been harshly shaken, and we may hope that, far from being broken, they are being forged afresh, perhaps stronger than before.

For never before have these writers made plain to one another the vital importance to them of each others' statements and thoughts about the great ordeals of current history.

Truth is difficult. Sometimes it hides itself so well that, even after a long lapse of time, it is hard to be altogether certain of possessing it. And after all, for a writer, it is perhaps more imperative to seek it than to find it. Whoever sincerely seeks the truth is already *in* the truth.

The Soviet and French writers have written to each other, they have told each other what they think is true; no doubt they will not be able to convince one another until they have met, until they have been able jointly to bring together the same evidence and the same elucidations about the Hungarian tragedy. But what is already apparent, what is essential, is that none of us has doubted the sincerity of the others, and I think even – is it not so? – that our mutual esteem may emerge reinforced from the ordeal.

Is it not strange and marvellous that it should be precisely at the heart of our contradictions that the first really close and powerful relations between us should thus be born? But after all, is that not also what dialectic teaches us?

Is it not strange and marvellous that a Hungarian writer, crushed by misfortune and, like you, sure that his French friends are mistaken, sure that the revolution has been saved, not broken, by the Red Army, should address to us these noble words: 'We have suffered a great deal, but at the same time learned a great deal, and first and foremost not to consider as a bandit the man who does not share our opinion. We hope that the French intellectuals understand with what deep feelings of friendship we await their help.'

These words will, I am sure, echo for a long time in the hearts of many French writers. They will do more, I am sure, than the best of arguments to make them secretly reflect. Nothing brings people together more than confidence. We partisans of Peace saw this when the National Council, which opened on Saturday in an atmosphere of mistrust and division, ended on Sunday in unity. And in enthusiasm for having recovered unity, and this although nobody had abandoned one jot of his convictions.

And that is so true, my dear Ilya Ehrenburg, this mutual confidence has such power, that today I can write to you something which, even a few days ago, I thought would be impossible for many weeks to come, perhaps many months: I was afraid that that exhibition of French art, which, before these tragic events, you had asked me to come to the Soviet Union to open in the name of the Friends of France, would have been put off till later – much later. A journey to Moscow, when feelings on both sides, the feelings of my Soviet friends as well as those of my French friends, were painfully opposed, seemed to me postponed to a distant future. But now, suddenly, this is not so. The thing seems to me once again possible, without any danger of such a journey being interpreted in a way that would be regrettable to either side. Without our going back on what we think about the tragic events which have opposed us, the disagreement can now be transfigured into a virile friendship of the kind that is tempered afresh by trial. That, at least, is what I personally feel at this moment. It seemed to me, as I heard you, and as I read Béla Illés today, that I heard once more the echo of those words and their promise.

.   .   .   .   .

Three of the letters I received as a result of this publication called for special attention from me.

The first of them pointed out what appeared to be an error: had I not confused Béla Illés (from whom I quoted a few words), an opportunist and Stalinist writer of mediocre reputation, with Gyula Illyès, a writer of world reputation and one of the spokesmen of the insurrection?

I had in fact more or less confused them (knowing neither the one nor the other well). But was it not strange that my attention was drawn to this confusion as though it weakened my argument, whereas the same words, if they came from an insurgent, would have lost all value as an example in that context? I replied:

12 December 1956

Monsieur L. G——,

I found your letter on my return to Paris.

I had in the meantime learned of my confusion concerning Gyula Illyès.

But I do not think that this confusion alters the sense of what I wrote, and you seem to have misunderstood this.

The sense of my quotation is this: '*Even a Stalinist* writer (whether called Illyès or Illés, for, being as ignorant of Illés's position as a Hungarian writer might be of mine, I had attributed that of Illyès to him) – even a pro-Stalin writer who believes that we are wrong addresses friendly words to us and not, as formerly, insults, and this gives us a favourable impression of his sincerity.' It was not, as you seem to interpret it: 'If a liberal writer like G. Illyès believes in the justification of the Russian intervention, that will make us go back on our own convictions.'

Nothing in my letter, if you read it correctly, constitutes a repudiation of my earlier statements: it is, on the contrary, a way of 'taking note' of the apparent new dispositions of Soviet writers, with a view to a sincere search for the truth on their side as on ours – a way of 'committing' them perhaps more than they wish. . . .

I read also, in Paris, the appeal of which you sent me an extract, and here is the result: the C.N.E. has just, at my express request, telegraphed to the Soviet writers to invite them to join their efforts to ours with regard to the Hungarian writers, in particular the writers who have been arrested or have vanished.

I think this information will have enlightened you as to the exact significance of my efforts in the midst of this whirlwind of contrary passions, from which I am trying to keep aloof.

The second letter came from the Association of Hungarian Writers, which at that time was not dissolved, nor even yet suspended as it was a month later.

It pointed out to me the same mistake as between Illés and Illyès. But chiefly it expressed uneasiness about the position I had taken up with regard to Soviet Russia, and in consequence, so they thought, with regard to the Hungarian writers. I answered them at once:

5 January 1957

Hungarian Writers Association,
Budapest.

You have done me the honour of writing personally to me. I must, therefore, deduce that what I have said or done in reference to the Hungarian tragedy seems to you not without consequence. And also that on this point you feel, with regard to me, worried or disturbed. For this reason I should like to explain my position clearly.

My whole life as a writer is organized around a centre of gravity which has never moved and never will move as long as I have a brain to think with: the search for truth. I say 'search'. I make no claim to possess the truth. Anyone who makes that claim merely proves thereby that error is the air he breathes. Truth is not an object one can possess or a place one can live in.

It is the star that guides one but remains inaccessible. To put it even better, truth is a *way*. The man who takes truth as the foundation of his spiritual and moral life will be on the road all his life; if he stops, if he thinks he can stop, that is the end of him.

For ten years, in my relations as a writer with politics I have thus been fighting on two fronts: for Socialism, and against deceit within Socialism.

Against the lies of the enemies of Socialism I have no need to fight specially: I am fighting them by fighting for it. That is no problem.

It is a problem – and always a difficult one, often a painful one – to struggle against lying when it occurs within one's own camp. Because to do so may sometimes look like attacking the very cause one is defending. But the honour of a writer consists in being able to take that risk too, as you know better than I.

Ten years ago the hero of one of my stories cried: 'Whoever deceives the people cuts himself off from it. And if the people understands that it is being lied to, what confidence can it still have in the struggle? How can it be sure that it has really fought for the sacred aims that were proclaimed – since it is being lied to?' I wrote that before the great Budapest trials. Before Rajk's extorted confessions. I had written, even earlier: 'Every lie demoralizes the people a little more: helps its faith to decay. Social dislocation has set in.' The revolt of the Hungarian people, ten years later, brought tragic confirmation of these prophecies.

I recall this, my dear friends, not in order to exult over having been a prophet, but that you now may read what I am about to say to you in the same light.

The Hungarian people have been deceived. When you understood this, you courageously took part in opening its eyes. The burdens and hardships, which it endured with a firm heart while its Socialist faith supported it in its effort, became unendurable to it in the midst of imposture. It revolted against *lies*, as much as, and more than, against its sufferings. That is the admirable and exemplary thing about this revolt; and which will always be to your honour, because you expressed it.

But that is also what makes the revolt now not without danger.

May I, who write to you quietly in a well-warmed house in the heart of a peaceful countryside, say that? I would certainly not dare to do so, if you had not taken me as a witness; if I did not therefore owe it to you to reveal all that I think.

Deceit has decayed the faith of the Hungarian people. The liars are the real criminals. But a decayed faith is still a danger to the people it deserts. What such a people needs most urgently – more perhaps than coal and steel – is to find once more the healthy and firm bases for its activity and its future.

That largely depends on you. You have unveiled and fought the crime. You have now to show where justice and truth reside.

And it is just and true to say, as you do, that the revolt of the Hungarian people is not, has not been and does not intend to be a reactionary rebellion. To claim the contrary is dishonest, or, if sincere, a disgraceful error. And it is just and true, on your part – on this point our fraternal support will never fail you – to persevere in protesting against every attempt to throw doubt on this reality.

But it would not be just, it would not be true to let it be thought that there has not been, that there is not a danger, a great danger, of reaction. That danger exists at the heart of every decayed faith. Reactionary forces know this well, they know well that they have no better ally than popular despair. And they know detestably well how to exploit it. It would be neither true nor just to pretend to ignore this.

Such exploitation has happened in Hungary. It is happening still. Does it in any way justify the Soviet military intervention? I continue to think that it does not: it would confirm, if there were need of confirmation, that this intervention was a grave error, since it has precipitated and aggravated the despair and, with it, the danger of the reaction it was attempting to stifle. But we are not disputing about the past – that will be the task of the historians. We have to discuss the present and the future.

You have shown and are showing by your constancy,

courage and proud tenacity, that the Hungarian revolution remains, in your view, firmly committed to the course of Socialism. And with all our hearts we believe you. You denounce the peril of a return of the inhuman practices which the revolt has swept away. And with all our hearts we approve you. But you do not (to our knowledge) show that you are conscious of the risks Socialism has run, or vigilant towards the risk it is still running. It would reassure us to hear you say you were. To hear you denounce *also* the peril Socialism has passed through, and point out *also* the traps that are still laid in the shadow of misfortunes. It would reassure us if you no longer passed over in silence (even though this silence seems to you provisionally justified by the need to put first things first) what has happened and is still happening in Hungary to the disadvantage of Socialism. It would reassure us if you showed your clear-sightedness today, as before. To know that the Hungarian people can still be sure you will tell it the *whole* of what is just and true – the whole, even including things it might not like to hear just now; sure of no longer being even a little deceived – even by silence. The fullest light is necessary.

And it is that, indeed, my dear friends, it is that light that we are also asking of our Soviet colleagues. Their truth may be astray at present, it is caught in an opposite kind of trap; but I refuse to doubt that the just and the true will finally win the day with them, as with us all. For my part, I will do my best, for them and with them, in this obstinate search. In the long run it is inconceivable that we shall not, sooner or later, all meet again, advancing along the same road: the long, adventurous road, often hard to find, but at whose end the star beckons us.

.   .   .   .   .

The third letter came from a historian, an old man and an old friend of mine, whose letters periodically punctuated, as it were, nearly every action of mine, and whose esteem I value.

He sent me a copy of a letter he had just written to a young Communist woman who in bewilderment had asked him what she ought to do. ('One must never,' he wrote, 'yield and take the line of least resistance;

*when one thinks one is right, one must fight for that right to prevail.
Fight, fight, fight.')*

Above all, he was worried by my departure for Moscow:

'*Let us hope you will find in Moscow men with the will and the
power to "seek the truth sincerely". Meanwhile a people is being
assassinated.*'

27 December 1956

To M. J. T——,

Thank you for having sent me a copy of your letter to
a Communist friend.

I don't think I would change a word in it, for after all –
though not a Communist – for the last ten years I have been
following your advice, against wind and tide (winds and tides
from both sides . . .) and I am going on. My journey to Moscow
(if it takes place) will have no other meaning. It is already a
somewhat sensational progress that men like me should have
obtained, on the occasion of the Hungarian tragedy, the
publication in the *Literaturnaya Gazeta* of *our protest textually.*
And that we should have been answered there – even if the
answer is still all impregnated with old Stalinist reflexes. This is
the first time that the young people at the universities will have
been able to read in the Soviet Press a charge against their
Government – signed by friends of the U.S.S.R. whom they
know to be so. Whatever happens afterwards, this will have
taken place and cannot be deleted. It seems to me that it has
at last been possible to get the end of the lever under the
enormous mass that has to be raised. We must, above all, not
let go now. That is why I shall go to Moscow – with neither
too much nor too little confidence: because I must.

*I intended, as soon as I reached Moscow, to ask for a meeting at
Rostov House – everyone is familiar with the excellent reconstruction
of it at the beginning of the film* War and Peace: *it is now the
headquarters of the Union of Soviet Writers.*

I had even prepared my speech. But I did not make it.

*From the first words I exchanged with some of the Moscow writers
who are my personal friends, I realized that my speech, far from*

G

*making it possible for constructive relations to follow, would produce
quite the opposite effect: I should be shutting the gates in front of me.*

*I publish it here, however, so as to keep to my intention of showing
things as they are, not as one would like them to be. The reader will see
what it was that I could not say to the writers as a group, if I wished to
get a hearing from them afterwards. What I was able to say to them,
at first in private, and then before a number of them, will be found
further on.*

I am not speaking in my own name only. I am here to some
extent as a spokesman of a large number of fellow-writers. And
I am in a way deputed to let you know of their worries, as well
as mine.

The most important of the questions I have to put to you is
not so much the Hungarian business, although it is mainly
because of that that I am speaking to you. But the most important thing, I repeat, is not the question of who is wrong or
right – the future and history will say that – it is whether our
relations as writers and men of culture still have a real chance
of continuing and developing. And that is something we can
only find out in conditions of the greatest clarity and the greatest
frankness.

I shall therefore tell you frankly what it is first of all essential
for my fellow writers and myself to know. I mean, if we are not
mistaken about one another. My fellow writers and I have a
certain idea of the part which a writer has to play in the building
of Socialism, in the struggle for its triumph in the world, and it
is necessary for us to know if this idea is also yours. If it is not,
this will certainly not mean that we shall become adversaries,
or even indifferent. The friendship of the French progressive
writers towards the Soviet writers is, and will remain, very great,
even if we are not in agreement. During many years our professional relations were practically non-existent, and yet the
friendship remained. It will, I hope, never be threatened. And
if we were forced to conclude from our conversations that our
ideas are too far different for fruitful discussion, we should at
worst go back to the *status quo ante*, to the simple but firm friendship a doctor may have for a violinist: they have not much in

common to say to each other about their professions, but they are none the less great friends. Naturally that would be a great pity for the relations between our two cultures, and I hope with all my heart that it will not turn out so; but I have taken this precaution in order that it may be possible for us, on both sides, to speak without reserve, without fear to involve the friendship. For, I repeat, what we most need is clarity.

What idea, then, have we, the French writers fighting for Socialism, of the part we must play in this fight? I am not speaking of our part as authors of novels, poems or essays; I am speaking of the part we have to play at the heart of social and political events. This is an essential question, because it admits of two answers, which are very different and even to some extent opposed – not that this classes us in adverse camps, but still they are sufficiently far apart to make conversation difficult if not impossible.

One of these ideas, in fact, is that the rôle of men whose job is to use their brains to think, as that of the fitter is to use his hands to file, is to help the builders of Socialism more strictly to collect the elements by means of which they can check the rightness of their actions and avoid as far as possible errors and deviations. The first duty, obviously, of those who share this idea is to refuse to accept as true anything they have not themselves judged to be true, on sufficient evidence.

The other idea is, on the contrary, that the writers' first duty is to place all the authority of their names at the service of the men of action who are building Socialism. The only truth they recognize is the truth of the builders, and they forbid themselves to judge it. They become willingly its mouthpieces, they make themselves the unconditional defenders of a truth which they have not contributed towards establishing.

These two ideas, I repeat, have each of them their merits and justifications – it is not for me to judge which is the better – but it must be admitted that they are irreconcilable. What valid exchange could there be between a man who takes as his first task the personal search for truth and a man who makes himself the mouthpiece of a government? No more than between him and that government itself. There is no longer a relation of equal to equal, and any discussion is from the start doomed to sterility.

Of the drama of this contradiction we have ample experience in France. I have known it better than anyone. It is even, in a way, my personal drama. I have no need to tell you that I am a man of the first idea – the one that requires the writer to pass every truth presented to him through the sieve of his reason and to accept as true only what he himself has recognized as such. This is what for ten years has set me against my Communist friends. But for a year now, since the revelations made during the Twentieth Congress, it has become the drama of many Communist comrades as well. When the Rajk trial took place, I wrote that I could not believe in the truth of the trial and that Rajk, his judges and other men above them, were lying. Two Communist writers, joint editors at that time of the *Lettres Françaises*, assured me I was wrong. They talked to me for five hours, but failed to convince me, for they brought me no further argument except the one I have mentioned: 'It must be the truth because the builders of Socialism say so, in Moscow, in Budapest, and in Paris. What right have we not to believe them? And by what right do you cast doubt on their word and ours?' It was no good my answering: 'By the right I have to judge for myself' – the idea was too much contrary to theirs. But Rajk was rehabilitated. The horror of the crime and the deceit aroused revolt among the Hungarian Communist writers and many French Communist writers, among them the first of those two who had spoken to me, but not, it seems, the other. Which shows clearly how far these two mental families are foreign to each other. The first believed, like the second, that the truth of the builders of Socialism was really the only truth, but when it turned out that some of these builders had lied he at once lost this fine confidence, and now he has passed into the camp of those men who, like me, no longer accept truth without judging it. The second, on the contrary, does not seem to see in these tragic events any reason for changing. His total adherence to the builders of Socialism makes him share with them good and evil, glory and opprobrium; to this he remains faithful, which is also courageous, and how should I blame him for it? I am still friends with him, as with the first; but while in future I can discuss things with the first, what useful discussion could I still have with the other?

What is already true as between French writers is even more true as between French and Soviet writers. Are we on the same side of the barricade or are we separated? It is necessary to know this definitely, and I must admit to you that we are uneasy. For the last year we have been asking ourselves some very grave questions. You too have defended for many years, like the two writers of whom I spoke, certain official truths which you forbade yourselves to doubt. I remember when I came to Moscow three years ago, for the first time, on the way back from China. In the course of a discussion with some of you I complained that the Soviet writers had not aided their French colleagues, when these were contending with the attacks of the reaction on the occasion of the affair of the 'murderers in white overalls'. A single phrase from you, I told them, a single word in formal condemnation of anti-Semitism, would have reduced to silence that band of jackals on our heels. 'But,' they answered me, 'how could we have done so? Do people defend themselves against a charge of being cannibals? That almost amounts to admitting that they could be. Anti-Semitism no longer exists in the U.S.S.R. any more than cannibalism.'

Today you know that the truth was not as simple as that, that there was anti-Semitism, that the Yiddish writers were being decimated and that appalling deportations of Jews have taken place on Soviet soil. You know many other things as well. That a great many crimes have been committed in secret or under cover of lies. You cannot, I am sure, think of Isaac Babel, of Platonov, or of Boris Pilniak without pain and humiliation. And it is true, all that is in the past. But, as the saying goes: if a man deceives you once, shame on him. If he deceives you twice, shame on you. How, therefore, could the attitude of the second of the writers I mentioned reassure me? What guarantee is he taking that he will not be deceived again? Since he himself proclaims that he will continue to believe, unreservedly, in the truth of the Party. Without allowing himself to judge it. Since he accepts afresh without judging it – and here we come to the crux of the matter – the official Soviet truth about the Hungarian affair?

There are many of us, as you know, who have taken a stand against the intervention of the Red Army. Whether we were wrong or right is another issue. The important issue here is that of our attitudes towards that tragedy. The men on my side, those who share my idea, have been ceaselessly, during the last three months, collecting the evidence for judgement. Not, believe me, as part of a kind of intellectual game, which the enormity of the events would render decidedly absurd. They are doing it because they have never ceased, all their lives, to be convinced, with Lenin, that the truth is revolutionary. And that error and lying are, even more surely, counter-revolutionary. We have certainly seen this at Budapest. Ten years ago I wrote that deceiving the people would lead – on the day when the people found out – to hurling it into doubt and into despair, and, in consequence, into the arms of reaction. It is no pleasure to me, you may be sure, that events in Hungary have so quickly and so terribly proved me right; but what lesson are people learning from this? That is what alarms me – and many others besides me. You wrote to us, you answered our protest – and although what you wrote was only what we had already to a large extent read and been told about the so-called Fascist *putsch* which had been crushed, we felt considerable hope as we read your words. It was natural that we should have some information, and you other information. We were going to be able, we thought, to compare them. Ignazio Silone wrote to Sholokhov to suggest an exchange of documents. A great many of us have replied to you, giving you our arguments. And we have been waiting for what you would have to say to us, in your turn. We have waited for a long time, at first with confidence and then with uneasiness. We have waited in vain. Your answers never came.

What are we to conclude? There have been graver things. From the first day we were alarmed on behalf of our Hungarian colleagues. Even Aragon, even the Communists, signed a telegram to the Kadar Government asking for an assurance that they would be safeguarded. We got no reply. We telegraphed again. And we telegraphed to you as well. We asked you to associate yourselves with us for the defence, in the whirlwind of events, of all those men of culture. The only reply that reached us, the only reply to all those telegrams, was the brutal suspension of the Union of Hungarian Writers and the arrest of a great number of them. Those writers, you see, may really have committed evil actions – I am not discussing that, because I know nothing about it, any more than you do. But if we had had a reply from the Kadar Government, or if you had told us: 'Yes, we will see that the Hungarian writers be assured of justice,' we should be less uneasy today, for we would be able to say to ourselves that those who have none the less been arrested have doubtless deserved it. But that silence and *your* silence remind us of the silence that surrounded Isaac Babel, Koltsov and Meyerhold, and we are not happy. If Lukacs, Tardos, and Gyula Hay are released without any intervention from you, or if one day they are rehabilitated after their death, and you have been deceived a second time, what will you think then? As you see, it would be impossible to speak to you more frankly than I am doing, or more directly. And I repeat: whatever may be your response to all this, it will not jeopardize our friendship. You have the right to have chosen differently from us, and we have not the right to reproach you for that. But I repeat, also, the point is, whether exchanges have really become possible. It would really be no good discussing the Hungarian affair if you were bound to refuse to listen to our arguments, and bound to stick to the official truth without giving an inch, as those two writers did with me at the time of the Rajk trial. You will tell me that we can talk about many other things, about which in any case we can agree: Tolstoy, Dostorevsky and Stendhal. Certainly. But I will reply to you frankly: we have no desire to, at this moment. At this moment, for us, it is the whole future of Socialism that is at stake. At stake in every way. For it has received some harsh blows in many countries, and first and foremost in our own, where the reaction is at present winning, over a people that has lost its bearings, a greater victory than it has won for a very long time; where the popular front, which at the beginning of last year we felt to be within reach, has vanished in the ashes and the smoke of Budapest. But Socialism is at stake, above all, in our hopes. Crimes, lies, injustices and the use of force – we know of course that there is no revolutionary struggle that can altogether escape these. Especially when it has been going on for nearly half a century, doubtless will go on for as long again, and is spreading over the surface of the globe. But when these crimes and lies burst open, when they bleed and fester under our fingers, we feel the need to be reassured. To be assured that these are only accidents, not accepted methods. Not indelible warts on the face of tomorrow which, if they multiply, will in the end make it monstrous. And how are we to be reassured unless, outside of official truth, we can discuss this man to man, by the feeble light at our disposal – yet it is a light which very many other men, I assure you, are anxiously waiting for, as though for a few drops of cool water in their great thirst? Tolstoy and Balzac cannot slake them. You and we, for the moment, are the water carriers. If my friends and I remain alone we shall not get far. If, on the contrary, you help us, if I bring back to France the assurance I have been able to discuss with Soviet writers, openly and freely, the great problems that obsess us, then we shall shut up all those wild beasts who, ever since the tragic month of November, have been howling with evil joy, and we shall comfort those unfortunate Frenchmen who, in their hundreds of thousands, had placed all their faith in Socialism and are now wondering, in pain and torment, whether they have still the right to give it their confidence.

.   .   .   .   .

I decided, as I have said, not to make this speech, but one must not draw any too extreme conclusions from this.

What I renounced saying to the writers at a professional meeting I did say to them in private, or in small friendly groups – I said that and still more to them, during the three weeks of my visit.

Notes were taken during these conversations, and these I will not reproduce: not that they seemed to me to contradict in the slightest degree what I have just written, but because the arguments used on one side or the other would tell the reader nothing that he does not know already from many polemical writings published on this subject. I do not want this dossier *to become more boring than is necessary. I will confine myself (by way of example) to publishing what in general served me as a concluding statement – and was also, fairly generally, recognized by my opposite numbers as an acceptable approximation.*

I think the score, on balance, is rather gloomy.

Before November 4th: The Soviet Union was winning on all counts. It had emerged victorious from the cold war, had reconstituted the unity of the Socialist camp by bringing Yugoslavia back into the fold, had established its prestige as far as India and Indonesia, had subjected the Middle East to its influence by pacific means, had carried its cultural 'offensive' into the heart of the *bourgeois* world, and had disarmed anti-Soviet propaganda by an unprecedented courage in redressing past errors.

After November 4th: Nehru has again become distant, the Middle East is divided, Yugoslavia has been thrown back to the other side, the Socialist camp is split by cracks which it takes intervention by the Chinese to fill in, the cultural offensive is blocked, the hostile propaganda is flaring up as it did in its best days, and the Communist Parties in the *bourgeois* democracies are everywhere in a state of crisis.

At this price, order has not even been fully restored in Hungary, and from the Elbe to the Danube the threats of war have not been extinguished.

If Hungary remains for too long a country where Socialism is imposed by constraint upon a reticent population engaged in a muffled struggle against its Government and the occupying army, this population will want to be delivered, by war if necessary. What is being built up in Hungary at present is, I fear, not Socialism but resistance. It is possible that, for lack of hope, this resistance may decay and grow discouraged. That will not be a victory. It will be an infected wound at the heart of Socialism, just as Franco's Spain is at the heart of a capitalist world. Each of the two is an element of decomposition in its own camp.

It seems to me that your efforts, like ours, should be directed towards doing everything to avoid such a decay.

In consequence, in so far as the insurrection was formed around the Hungarian writers, we should, as a matter of the greatest urgency, renew contact with them—if not fraternal, at least confraternal.

That, essentially, is what I came here to tell you.

.   .   .   .   .

By way of conclusion and although I had not asked for anything of the kind, a big meeting of writers was organized to hear me. I prepared on that occasion a new speech, in terms, as I thought, sufficiently 'diplomatic' to make it possible for a not entirely sterile discussion to be set going.

In the three weeks I have been here, I have had a great many meetings with many people, writers and others. And I have come to understand many things. In particular, I have come to understand that, while the French writers reproach their Soviet friends with their silence, these reproach their French friends with claiming to pronounce something like a judgement upon them. They do not admit that their French colleagues should claim to judge them. And so what I should like to establish immediately, in order to make this completely clear and to avoid any misunderstanding, is that there never, I am convinced, enters the head of any French progressive writer the incredible idea that he might be a judge of anyone. Not that this is the first time we have been accused of setting up as judges. After the Liberation, Jean Paulhan and his friends made the same reproach against us. The truth is that there is, among the French writers, a tradition which dates from Voltaire and even before, and which caused I forget now which Austrian or German statesman to exclaim: 'When an innocent man's foot is trodden on anywhere in the world, the Frenchman cries out!' In the mouth of that statesman this was said perhaps with exasperation, and it meant, no doubt: 'What is this mania the French have, of always meddling in what does not concern them?' But I must tell you that this French tradition is in fact so strong that, as far as I am concerned, I have never been able to take that jibe as anything but a compliment, which has always filled me with pride.

For this reason no doubt it is no accident that it should be a French writer who, for many years, in a way represented the conscience of the world. I mean Romain Rolland. Could it be said of Romain Rolland that he was ever a judge? He was far too human, he knew human nature far too well, ever to dare to judge other men, but he did judge men's actions, and when these were unjust he cried out, and his voice was listened to by the whole world. The difficulties which have arisen after the tragic events of November between the French and Soviet writers do not show that one side has presumed to judge the other: they show merely, alas, that no voice in the world has yet replaced that of Romain Rolland, and that its absence makes itself painfully felt. For I imagine that, if Romain Rolland had said to the French progressive writers: 'It is you who are wrong,' he would have spared many of us some painful debates within our consciences. But I imagine, also, that if, on the contrary, he had said that to the Soviet writers, it would have had more effect on their minds than anything Jean-Paul Sartre could write, or I, or any of your friends. That must recall us to humility, if there was need of that. On the other hand, it seems to me that if Romain Rolland had tirelessly and relentlessly demanded news of Lukacs, for instance, or if he had insisted on a meeting with him, his voice would not have fallen into the well of silence into which ours has fallen. And no doubt many things would have been elucidated, which are not yet so, because we, alas, have not the same moral authority as Romain Rolland. Once more, I say all this to you to show you that, if ever the idea of judging the Soviet writers had occurred to any of us, the mere memory of Romain Rolland would immediately have recalled him to more modest feelings.

You will believe me, therefore, when I repeat that any idea of judgement is basically absent from the intentions of the French progressive writers. Only, it is equally absent with regard to the Hungarian writers. We do not allow ourselves to judge the Hungarian writers any more than the Soviet writers. But I am not sure that the Soviet writers maintain the same attitude with regard to their Hungarian colleagues. It has seemed to me that they sometimes allowed themselves to pass a judgement, and a judgement that was often severe. And I know that the Hungarian writers themselves have the same impression, and that they feel bitterly about it. The same sort of bitterness as some of you feel towards your French colleagues when you think you are being judged by them. And so, at the end of my visit here, I tell myself that one of the most urgent things is certainly to re-establish between all of us the brotherly confidence that must exist between men who have not always the same opinion about events, but who have not for that reason the right to become judges of one another. I have already told several of my friends here how desirable it seems to me that contacts should be established afresh between the writers of all countries, and first and foremost those of Hungary and the Soviet Union. But that these contacts were only conceivable apart from any spirit of judgement or accusation – that they must, on the contrary, take place in a spirit of mutual under-standing and information. I should be happy to hear your opinion on this.

Naturally it seems to me no less urgent that contacts should be re-established between the Soviet and the French writers. But as I have already explained to some of you, certain con-ditions are necessary for that. I have no need to tell you that these conditions are not my own, because I am here, because I have personally re-established them without waiting for the conditions to be fulfilled. But my reason for coming was precisely, in the first place, to inform you. It would be no good for us to join in desiring the resumption of contacts between French and Soviet writers, without my informing you as to what can make that possible – or, on the contrary, difficult at the present time.

I must, therefore, tell you that one preliminary condition seems to me to be that the French writers should first receive from you the replies for which they are waiting. You wrote to us to give us your arguments, we wrote to you in our turn to give you ours, and we were already congratulating ourselves that the dialogue had started again, and, what is more, had started again in these difficult circumstances. And we were awaiting your reply with an enormous interest. But it did not come. We had also written to you to ask you to join with us in order to see that the Hungarian writers, in the considerable difficulties in the midst of which President Kadar would have to govern, should not be the victims of these difficulties, which, as history shows, always result in certain inevitable injustices. But we have had no response to this, either. If the atmosphere in French intellectual circles has not changed since my departure six weeks ago, I think that those are two things on which the French progressive writers would first of all wish to hear you express yourselves. After that, I think, everything will become easier.

That is what, I think, it was essential to say to you; and now I think the most useful thing would be for you, in your turn, to ask me all the questions that will seem to you necessary, as frankly as I have just done.

.   .   .   .   .

What came of this suggestion will be found below, in a sort of report which I published in Le Monde, *a few weeks later, when I was back in France. It is, therefore, not necessary to repeat it here.*

MOSCOW COLLOQUIES[1]

Officially I went to the Soviet Union to open the Exhibition of French Reproductions of French Masters.

Substantially, I expounded the opposition views to its writers.

The Hungarian tragedy had raised, between them and us, a misunderstanding which threatened to solidify, and a new Iron Curtain. Should we allow this to fall once more, without even moving a finger? My first impulse had been to suspend the Exhibition, to refuse to go, and to put forward as a preliminary condition for any resumption of contact a meeting in Budapest with the Soviet writers.

[1] Published in *Le Monde* on 12 and 13 May 1957. A certain number of cuts made by me to reduce the article to publishable length have been restored here.

A calmer, more serious examination of that tragic situation led me, later, to think that such a condition could not for a long time be fulfilled: because it was obviously unrealizable for them (they do not claim the same independence as we do) and for us (we should not be allowed to penetrate into Hungary).

It was also quite obvious that there was a new political 'frost' in Moscow. From various cries of alarm and appeals for the maintenance of the links with the West, forged with such difficulty, there transpired the agonized fear of a fresh isolation. It was absurd, by breaking off relations from our side (unless we were firmly set on a pure and simple return to the cold war), to encourage the 'extremists' against the democratic elements, instead of helping these in their efforts towards internal emancipation and external *rapprochement*.

None the less, when I decided to take up the abandoned plan, I was not free from apprehension. Was it not a mistake on my part? Would not my going to Moscow be interpreted there, contrary to my intentions, as a kind of assent? Would there not be at least an attempt to exploit it in that sense?

If these apprehensions were justified, was I not running the risk, in case my visit there ended in a failure, of doing more harm than good? If I came back empty-handed, would I not have ruined even more, and for a long time to come, any chance of appeasement, not to mention reconciliation?

Now I am home again. I had honestly vowed to myself that on my return I would publish the results whatever they might be. This is what I am about to do. With all the objectivity of which I am capable. They are not sensational results. They are still on many points disappointing. And yet they open the door, I believe, to constructive relations. But the reader will judge of this.

I must begin by acknowledging the way in which I was received. My fears were groundless: while I was shown, by a thousand kindnesses, that they appreciated the proof of friendship represented by my going there in such difficult circumstances, I was spared, with the greatest discretion, anything that might have been painful to me in such circumstances. There were no big receptions, speeches, Press conferences – in a word, no orchestration to exploit my presence there for propaganda purposes or political ends. I might have feared, also, that my position as a guest, luxuriously lodged and fed and transported, would make it difficult for me to refuse this or that conventional or conciliatory statement which the newspaper reporters would try to extract from me. I did not have to refuse them, for I was not asked for them. I expected at least, in the course of my conversations, to have to defend my opinions about the events, to see them submitted to a battering, to be subjected to intensive propaganda, and to be asked to transmit to my French friends, on my return, the things that had been said to me. Nothing of the sort. On the contrary, I always found myself face to face with 'defenders' explaining to me why *they* must think as they did, even if, unfortunately as they said, the point of view in France was different.

Finally, if I escaped all these other things, I had serious doubts as to whether, in any case, I should be given many opportunities for informing Soviet opinion of these divergencies of view. Even on this point my mistrust was mistaken. Far better – every opportunity was offered to me: interviews, radio, television; my statements were faithfully reproduced and, on the radio and on television, I spoke 'live', and so without any censoring. Of course they trusted me, I imagine, to behave as a decent foreign guest. But no pressure was ever brought upon me. A long discussion in the circle of the Foreign Library was recorded complete and broadcast a few days later. I am obliged to wonder if the French radio or television would, after the Suez affair, have allowed the same liberty to a Soviet writer. . . . In any case, as far as I am concerned, it is some years since I was free to speak either on our radio or, indeed, in the *Lettres Françaises. . . .*

All this should be borne in mind, I think, as a clearly favourable point. It seemed to me only honest to mention it at the start before going on to things less positive.

In the course of my conversations in the first days, a writer who was a friend of mine said to me: 'I am afraid you will go away empty-handed. I hope you will not go away empty-hearted.'

That was perhaps, taking everything into account, too pessimistic a view. But on the whole it proved sound.

If the essential question is held to be how far one may hope to make the Soviet writers go back on their opinion on the Hungarian affair, I must, in fact, reply: not at all. We shall never make them, in the slightest degree, let go of their profound conviction that the armed intervention in Hungary has saved peace. Neither they nor anyone over there – as far, of course, as I have been able to see for myself – is willing to doubt it: not even people who have suffered from the régime in the past and did not refrain, in my presence, from severe criticisms (rehabilitated people, clandestine poets). As far as my experience goes, it is a unanimous conviction. Nor is it a conviction held to order. Nor a consequence of a lack of information. In the course of my discussions I was quickly forced to perceive that to set out my arguments was absolutely superfluous: they all knew them, and as well as I did. Apart from the fact that the Western radio (chiefly the B.B.C.) is openly listened to, thousands of soldiers have told their story, and nobody affects to believe that they fired only on a handful of Fascists. That they were forced to fire on students and workers – all this is known to everyone, and everyone has been terribly shaken by it. Apart from a few 'extremists' who spoke to me of the Hungarians with antipathy and ill will, those I saw were men suffering from a deep wound. A wound with salt rubbed into it, for their first dead fell, they say, without defending themselves. They do not absolve themselves, however, and are for the most part fully conscious of the responsibility the Soviet Union bore for this popular rising. In spite of that, I met no one who would consent to doubt that the intervention had, in the last resort, become inevitable.

They do not and will not believe that, once the affair had started, it could have been stopped half-way as in Poland. They have no doubt that Hungary was about to pass – and very shortly – into the Western camp, lock, stock and barrel. Nagy would not have held out for a week. Since no one imagines that the Soviet Union could have tolerated the setting up of such a powder-keg in the heart of Eastern Europe, the armed intervention would have taken place, they say, sooner or later. Better sooner than later. Above all, for the peace of the world. No argument of any kind could, I fear, destroy this conviction in their minds. In any case, none of my arguments succeeded in doing so.

And yet, I repeat, this conviction is in no way an absolution. And I can bear witness that none of the writers with whom I talked (apart from the few 'extremists' whom I have mentioned) harbours with regard to his Hungarian colleagues feelings or judgements that are basically unjust. 'Let them at least,' that Hungarian writer who took refuge in the West said to me, 'let them at least repudiate the official line and stop treating us as Fascists! If only they consent to speak of us honestly, we could discuss things with them.' I think I can really assure them that this is the case. Men like Szabo, Peter Verès and Gyula Illyès still have the esteem of all and the profound affection of their friends. 'But in that case,' I asked one of them, 'why have you never written this, to them or to us?' 'The fact is,' he said, 'we would gladly have written to you again, after your reply. Unfortunately, while we were in agreement among ourselves on the essential, on all the rest we had opinions that differed too widely. We have not succeeded in harmonizing them.' 'Dammit!' I exclaimed, 'don't you understand that your disagreements would have brought you nearer to us?' 'Yes,' he said, 'but we don't like to show ourselves disunited. . . .' He said later: 'Perhaps also we lack initiative.'

Unfortunately that is true. But the causes of it seem to me complex, and not all of them negative. A man who is not a writer but lives in close contact with writers and knows their problems and who thanked me warmly for my presence, warned me none the less: 'You can do us a great deal of good,' he said to me, 'but also a great deal of harm. A great deal of good,' he explained, 'because the mere presence of a protester who is doubtless firm, but also friendly without any *arrière-pensée*, not only warms our hearts, but preserves or revives among us an atmosphere of conscientious discussion which is profitable to those who are fighting against obstruction by the "reactionaries".' (That is the name given to the hardened

H

Stalinites over there, whereas the others are called 'progressives'.) 'A great deal of harm because if you were to insist on too
much, if you were to repeat some statement which imperialist
propaganda might get hold of, you would make its author a
vulnerable target of the whole of our Press, which is still con-
trolled by the "hard core". And that would mean one of our
people *hors de combat* for a time.'

That throws light on the feelings the Soviet writers harbour
towards the Hungarians. 'But you,' I said to a very 'progressive'
writer – 'should not you understand your Budapest colleagues
better than anyone? Have you never said to yourselves that,
but for the grace of God, you might have been in their place?'
He exclaimed: 'But we were there!' He added: 'We are there
still. But we act differently.'

He compared his Hungarian colleagues to those 'new boys'
who, at a boarding school, instead of understanding the muffled,
patient struggle carried on by the 'old hands' against the
masters, upset the soup tureen or break the windows and so
revive, for a long time to come, a supervision which was
beginning to be less strict.

'This comparison,' he added, 'must not make you believe
in any weakening of our adhesion to the régime under the
direction of the Party. You must realize that, in spite of its
errors, our attachment remains irreducible. You should see the
first reason for the silence with which you reproach us in this
loyalty – in our repugnance to give the adversaries' calumnies
any handle. You have, in fact, understood clearly,' he said,
'because you wrote that, under the Occupation, none of you
ever denounced the errors of the Resistance, either – the mur-
derous rivalry between certain leaders, and their settlements of
accounts.' 'It is true,' I admitted, 'that we did not protest,
either, against Mers-el-Kebir or against the abandoning to the
enemy of the *maquis* of the Vercors.' He said: 'But in our
country all that has been going on much longer than four
years. . . .'

This obsession with the danger of serving the reaction (equal
in fact to our obsession, during the Resistance, with the danger
of serving Vichy and Nazism) has in the past certainly helped

in large measure to hold them back from plotting against tyranny. They cannot, without reversing their own judgements, approve of the Hungarians for not having shown the same scruples. But, today as in the past, this is certainly not the only feeling that restrains their tongue or their pen. It is a fact that they are still utterly weaponless since they don't control the Press. Weaponless and vulnerable. No longer personally, it is true, in their life or liberty: all fear of arrest has disappeared. To that, too, I can bear witness. During my first visit, in the autumn four years ago, I had already noted, as between the atmosphere I found and that described a year earlier by Michel Gordey, the same difference as between a travelogue and a thriller. But the conversations were still prudent and conformist. Two years later, speech had already become so free that a famous writer could ask me in public if one of my colleagues, also well known, was really honest – and this because of the way in which, having freely seen everything he wanted to see in the Soviet Union, he had written about that country on his return. . . . 'What?' I had asked uneasily. 'Did he speak so ill of it?' 'No, no!' he said. 'On the contrary! He finds everything in it all right! After all, not everything is going so well in our country! Is it honest to hide this?' And I had to explain that, in fact, we felt bound to refrain in France from the criticisms which we expressed openly before them, for fear of indirectly giving these as food to enemy propaganda. And as I write this today, I realize how well we ought to understand the fact that the Russians often feel bound to refrain from confiding to a foreigner the things they could, and still can, say among themselves.

I myself received a vivid proof of this. From the first days of my visit I was advised – and at first I did not understand why – not to ask to be allowed to speak to the writers as a group, as a constituted body. 'You will get nothing out of it.' When I had better understood the reasons for this advice I ceased to insist. And yet, probably, they were reluctant to appear to be running away, and on the eve of my departure some thirty writers received me, after all, in one of the rooms at their Union. One of them was Dudintsev, the author of *Not by Bread Alone*, the book most hotly discussed at present. In the last few days he has once more kicked over the traces – so much so that he has been called to order: he has therefore no lack of boldness or vigour. But on that day he did not say a word. Not a single one. Neither he nor nine-tenths of those present.

'The main thing,' one of my neighbours whispered in my ear, his intense satisfaction being evidently not diminished by their attitude, 'is not that they should reply, it is that they should have heard you!'

I had spoken, if not without diplomacy, at least without being mealy-mouthed. Two or three writers who occupy important positions in the Union, and with whom I had already had conversations, replied to me in a way which, indeed, seemed to me very frank and rather positive (especially about the opportuneness of meeting the Hungarian writers). The others remained silent. 'Well, comrades,' they said to these, 'your turn! We hope we shall not be the only ones to answer Vercors?' But they were the only ones. The only voice that was raised was that of an 'extremist', the editor of the review *Ogoniok*, who attacked me on the Egyptian affair: did I not think it would also be interesting if the French writers met their Egyptian colleagues? The hint was obvious. But it was too easy for me to reply that such a meeting would present no problem because *we* had protested against the Suez attack. The audience said nothing although one could feel that it disapproved of this hostile diversion. Fresh encouragements from their comrades were still in vain, and the silence became so painful – but I let it establish itself – that one of my hosts fired at me a purely literary question, as though the main discussion were exhausted – and everyone in fact behaved as though it were closed. Groups formed, and small conversations started, which would have been decidedly unflattering to me if they had not obviously meant: 'Understand that we shall say nothing.'

A fortnight earlier I would not have understood that one should see, in their reserve, first and foremost that form of prudence adopted by fighters who are anxious not to expose themselves in minor engagements when they must keep themselves in reserve for a long drawn-out campaign. Luckily I remembered the sentence of one of the first people I had spoken to, 'a great deal of good or a great deal of harm'; and indeed for several days already I had not been 'empty-handed'. Otherwise I should certainly have insisted. I think my insistance would have failed, and I should have brought back with me a very sad feeling.

.   .   .   .   .

'I am afraid you will go away empty-handed, I hope you will not go away empty-hearted.'

If I tried to report here all the things that had filled my heart gradually during the three weeks of my visit, before that last disappointing experience, I should never get to the end.

To speak only of the atmosphere, to begin with, I thought I found considerable progress in a great many fields. The streets were better lighted, more cheerful, with neon lighting in many colours, the shop windows wider, brightly lit, full of goods and more tastefully decorated. Also people were better dressed, and there was a wider range of stuffs. Motor traffic had at least doubled (we were more than once caught in traffic blocks, and in the centre parking is becoming a problem). The housing problem is still tragic. But the badly housed (most of my friends in Moscow are that) are now making plans: all of them know a friend or a relative who has just moved, and their turn will come. But there is no favouritism: one day a certain important figure in the Party and in the literary world invited me to a house-warming in the new flat just allotted to him; when the day came, somewhat crestfallen (but making the best of a bad job) he welcomed me in his old flat: on the day before the move a regulation had just been passed, giving priority to people worse housed than him. He will go on waiting.

I understood, at the same time, that one should see in the housing crisis, much more, I am convinced, than in shortage of merchandise, one of the major causes of the persistence of queues at the doors of all the shops (even including the antique shops and jewellers!). I had never before stayed long enough in Moscow to wander about as I did this time, beyond the main streets, through the small ones, nor realized before the absence in these *of any shop*, even in whole districts (an absence dating from when they were built, rather over a hundred years ago). How can the shops be decentralized and the thousands that are lacking be created, since to open a bakery would be to do away with two or three housing units? It is not possible to throw thousands of families into the street. Let us imagine Paris reduced to two big stores, a dozen *Uniprix* and a few big grocers, plus the Avenue de l'Opéra and a section of the Grands Boulevards, with some bits of avenues here and there – the rest practically without a shop. That will give some idea of the traffic in the few shopping streets – that crowd like an ant-heap at every hour of the day – and of the mob that would press into those excessively few big stores. Even a flood of merchandise would not solve the problem – on the contrary it would attract even more purchasers – it might even be said that it is a good sign when the queues and the mob increase.

For the first time I was able, a little bit, to live the life of a Muscovite. First of all, no doubt, because I was there for longer, but also, certainly, because some veils have been lifted. It is a fact that formerly people came to see me at the hotel, they did not receive me in their homes. Were they afraid of what the neighbours would say about these suspicious visits? Were they ashamed of unveiling the conditions of life in those communal apartments inhabited by several families? This time, in any case, there was nothing of the sort. They invited me to their homes without any reticence. I went there as I would have done in Paris. And yet I visited many people who, not long ago, must have been suspect to the régime and would have kept prudently at a distance from a compromising foreigner – and, what was more, one who had come to Moscow as a contradictor. . . . Not one of them, this time, suggested my taking the slightest precaution – as, for example, to come by taxi rather than in the Intourist car. Or again, to avoid the presence of interpreters. The criticisms and jokes that were uttered in their presence would not have been noticeably out of place in the offices of the *Canard Enchaîné*.

This expansive mood and freedom, so lacking at the meeting of writers which I have described, were quickly manifest in the same writers, when I met them a few at a time. What is more, I often had easier and more widely ranging discussions with them than with certain French Communists. Not one of them tried to get out of controversy: on the contrary, it was I, at first, who was reluctant to enter it, in spite of the direct or transparent invitations that were made to me (as for instance when one of them said casually he had argued with Carlo Levi for eight hours on end; and another broke a silence with the suggestion: 'Well, let's talk politics!'). The reserve, on my side, was not a tactical one, it was rather that, being received with such friendly warmth, I had not quite the courage to respond to these immediately with polemics and criticism. It was much easier at the second meeting, after having been able, at the first, to respond to friendliness simply with friendliness.

I had been told: 'You will see that there are differences between us, quite as great as your own.' This is doubtless not altogether true, since they are all agreed on the essential issue, which is, on the contrary, in France one of our points of disagreement, the intervention in Hungary. There is truth in it all the same. For on the *causes* of the intervention there is a wide range of views; all the way from the 'toughs', who throw the whole blame on to the Hungarians, to those who are most perplexed and keep asking themselves painfully: 'How can we have got to this pass? To be hated as we are?'

'They ought first to recognize their errors,' said one Soviet writer about his Hungarian colleagues when I urged him to meet them. Another, on the contrary, replied to me: 'Yes, we have been very wrong in not making contact with them. They are rather hot-heads, but they have not forfeited my esteem.' A third: 'Many of them are personal friends of mine. I am still friends with them, and I should like them to be with me. . . .' Another, with an expression of profound sadness: 'Oh, I can well imagine what they are thinking of us . . . and the impression our intervention must have made in France. . . .' Yet another: 'I am sure we would come to an understanding with them in ten minutes, but,' he added with a slight touch of ill humour, 'let the French not meddle with this: let them leave us to wash our dirty linen in private.' I remember, also, a rather terrible observation: 'You know, in Hungary, the living writers are not the *nec plus ultra.* . . . Just as here, it is the Communists who were persecuted, the purest are dead, you see. . . .' I had not the face to take up that 'just as here'. . . .

But even more than the Hungarian affair, it is the Twentieth Congress, with the wide range of its revelations, that has profoundly wounded them all. I saw men who had not yet recovered from it. Poems were read to me, which cannot be published but are circulated widely. Some of them are very moving: 'I have built on the sand', one of the finest of them confessed. 'We were building on granite, but now the stone is crumbling, splitting, subsiding under my feet. And yet I shall go on; I shall build, even on the sand, doggedly.' Another is addressed to the cowards who can come to terms with anything: 'The reptile, gliding, said to me: "To each his destiny." But as I watch him crawl, I know that that life is impossible.' Another, on the death of Stalin: 'It is night now. I wander through the town which lies silent, motionless, petrified under heavy dust. A street cleaner watches me pass. He is mute as those empty houses – as Socialism, which has now to be filled with living men.'

These are the cries of wounded men – and yet those most injured challenge our judgement: 'This is not your tragedy, it is ours,' they say. 'And has been for too long for us to accept your reproaches now. Yes, you yourself wrote: "It is not true to say we knew nothing", but you were almost the only one to speak out like that. It is really too easy to cry: "We have been deceived!" And to wash your hands with our soap. We kept silent? Was it keeping silence, to say, when questioned: "I cannot give you an answer"? If you content yourselves with such an answer and don't go further, does not that amount to covering up your eyes wilfully so as not to see – so as to keep your consciences at peace? Courage does not consist in serving a just cause when one believes it is spotless – everyone can do that; but in continuing to serve it even when it gets dirty. That is an old proverb with us.'

'Unfortunately,' I said to him, 'you did not always answer us in the way you say. . . .' And I reminded him of the conversation I had three years ago with a group of Soviet writers about anti-Semitism in their country. 'It is as unthinkable here as cannibalism!' they had answered me. Well, we know today that that wasn't true. 'Yes,' one of the writers present agreed. 'That was a lie.' Another shook his head. 'No,' he said thoughtfully. 'It was really unthinkable.' He sighed. 'And yet,' he said, 'it *was*.'

'In certain circumstances,' another writer said to me, 'the first duty may be simply to remain alive.' And he told me of the struggle which the survivors can carry on now, because they are alive, against the 'extremists', the profiteers of the régime whom the 'frost' had put in power and kept there, who intend to stay there and who attack every time they can. For instance, that ignoble article in *Krokodil* against a woman poet whom the old persecutions drove to suicide. Her poems were being published again; one of them was called 'Germany, my folly', a memory of her youthful years before 1914. The editor of *Krokodil* had picked out this poem in order to blacken the memory of its author by impugning her patriotism. But indignation was great among the 'progressive' writers, and the time past when the choice was between keeping silent or disappearing: a protest to *Krokodil* was covered with signatures.

I understood that at present it would be useless to ask more of them. Their Hungarian colleagues will be left to their fate. Officially at least – for, unofficially, people are worried about their future, and there is surreptitious action. I was given indirect but reassuring news of Lukacs. He is well and is working on a big book. His works, in fact, do continue to appear in the Soviet Union – a volume or two even in these last few weeks.

It is a muffled and difficult struggle, because at the same time loyalty to the Party – for the Communists, or simply to the Revolution, for the others – remains unconditional. 'Our friends had better be told, so that they may know where they stand, that we shall never break our solidarity with the Government and the Party,' one of the most famous, but also anguished, of the writers said to me. I had asked him if, in face of the terrible consequences by which he was still bruised, he did not regret the ruthlessness of the revelations which had made them possible. 'No,' he told me, 'even this brutal shock and its repercussions, even the Hungarian tragedy, are preferable to the long succession of mistakes and deceptions which a gradual evolution would have continued to drag along with it.' 'If they had happened could you not have denounced them to public opinion?' I suggested. He shook his head with a sort of fierce sadness: 'Never against my Party.'

This is not only the drama of Party members. It is, I think, that of all the 'progressives', whether they are Party members or not: the line of demarcation is the same, inside or outside. It is the drama of that woman intellectual who, at one time convinced (as all were) that Stalin was ignorant of the crimes committed in his name, told me, that I might understand her bewilderment: 'I am a loyal Soviet woman. But can you imagine what this means, to lose one's ideal?' 'But the Party,' I said to her, 'and all that?' She shrugged her shoulders slightly: 'The Party was Stalin, wasn't it?' 'In that case,' I asked, 'are you now sure that Stalin was really as he has been painted?' 'No,' she sighed, 'and that is the trouble: one no longer knows what to believe.' After a deep breath she said: 'It's a very great effort that has to be made now.'

The drama is less cruel among the young. The Stalin period has not marked them, has not impregnated their memories: childhood was extremely protected ('too spoilt!' I have heard it said), and the revelations of the Twentieth Congress have upset them less. They find it hard to imagine persecutions of which they knew nothing, in which perhaps they still only half believe, and they are inclined to judge their immediate elders severely, finding them pusillanimous. The under-twenty-fives get on better with the over-fifties, who have been less deformed by the period that has just passed. These are the two wings of 'progressivism'. The 'reaction' is in the centre, between thirty and fifty. It is not confined to members of the Party, but extends to most of the men in official positions, whatever they may be, who were formed by this period. The struggle for liberalization is also a struggle between generations.

These young people have never been afraid, are not afraid, and do not know what it means. I remember a meeting at the university, not very well attended, and with more than a sprinkling of foreign elements (I was invited by the French). The interpreter, after an exhausting day spent in translating, was no doubt rather tired. That evening she was interpreting rather less faithfully than usual. Perhaps also, unconsciously, some of my replies seemed to her to call for a little softening (I remember one unvarnished question: 'What do you think of the second intervention in Hungary?'). In short, her translations were sometimes rather toned down. But immediately the young Soviet students who understood French corrected them for their comrades. Not that they always agreed with my point of view, but because these opinions mattered to them and they wanted to know them in their full vigour.

This freedom of spirit, this absence of precautions or of prudence and circumspection, in contrast to the reserve shown by the writers as a group, seemed also to be found among the painters. No doubt for the same reasons: the painters rarely suffered personally, as the writers did – they have never run the same risks. The worst that happened to the most controversial ones was to be kept in the shade, to find earning a living difficult. Today they overturn, with a kind of joyous exuberance, those who yesterday oppressed them in the world of art and held the crown of the road. It seemed to me that people in France have no idea – or a very false idea – of what that Congress of Painters was like, at which I was present – the first to be held since 1918. Shepilov's intervention has, I think, been misunderstood, for lack of the full context. And yet, in the name of the Central Committee, he declared, in substance: 'All that is asked of you is to pay lip-service to Realism and the Party. That granted, paint as you like.' From the point of view of art, this is a total retreat which merely saves appearances. Socialist Realism becomes a kind of hold-all, and every good painting will be labelled as realist. And yet this prudent retreat seemed to those present hardly sufficient. The speeches showed this. In answer to a certain passage in the speech of the outgoing president, according to which the great classic painters, with a few exceptions like (he said) El Greco, had all been realists, one orator got a good laugh by saying: 'Don't let's despair of seeing, after Manet, poor El Greco rehabilitated in his turn.' Tomski, the sculptor, far from winning applause (as has been asserted) by his conformist report, was obliged to have it read for him by someone else: having been blackballed even as a delegate, he pleaded sickness and did not appear. One orator, just before the vote which was to elect or re-elect the ninety-nine members of the executive council, shouted: 'Don't vote for any of the out-going members! The doctors know that a cancer, if you leave the slightest grain of it in, will invade the whole organism again.' And in fact, *not a single one* was re-elected. This amounted to the complete crushing of the old tendency. The fact that, after that, the final resolution speaks of fidelity to realism under the enlightened direction of the Party amounts to no more than a mere stylistic flourish.

A few days before this, at the opening of our Exhibition, a man with a face like an old wounded lion rushed in on Ehrenburg's heels and mine, to be seen in the front rank before a picture by Cézanne, whom, only just before, he had been attacking in the Press with red-hot bullets as though Cézanne were alive. A woman behind him raised her hand in the air, saying: 'This hand glories in never having shaken that man's!' If I had not known what harm Alexander Gerassimov and his partisans have done to Soviet painters and painting, his last-minute attempts and his isolation would have excited my pity. But I am aware that he and his likes still have claws and teeth.

Yes, it is on the painting front that the *avant-garde* struggles are at present being carried on. Art serves as a pretext or cover for far deeper struggles. Some writer writes a pamphlet against a painter or a picture. Another writer answers him about the picture in question with a violence that is out of all proportion. And the first in his turn counter-attacks on the same subject, still more violently. Apparently the painting is still the only issue; but everyone knows very well what the real issue is.

I had a clear view of what was going on, simply in the case of our own exhibition. A hundred and twenty reproductions, from Corot to the present day – there was really nothing heinous about that. And yet, as though by chance, there was no gallery free to house it, except in an outlying district. But people came all the same, and the room never emptied. Painters came from Kiev to see Dufy and Rouault. Later it was announced that the Exhibition would go to Leningrad, after having been open for only a fortnight. There were such protests that the duration had to be doubled. During the first days visitors were admitted only up to five o'clock. 'If the object is to keep the workers away, let somebody say so!' The closing had to be postponed until eight in the evening.

At Odessa a student of applied mechanics at the Polytechnic Institute acquired, God knows how, some monographs on contemporary French painting and exhibited them in the corridors. Meetings followed which had such a success that the directors of the Institute became worried. A professor of mechanics was instructed to counter it. All the students were called together. Lantern slides of the masterpieces of Soviet art were shown on a screen. There were explanations and a panegyric. He was shouted at: 'Tell us about the others!' The poor man obviously could not. The director grew angry and said: 'Those who aren't satisfied, get out!' The whole audience rose and left. When I was in Moscow some of my friends were busy trying to get the student who had caused all the trouble reinstated, for the directors, after some hesitation, had thought fit to expel him.

At Leningrad a group of young people, coming out of the Picasso Exhibition at the Hermitage, looked for a room in which to hold a discussion. They were prevented. They tried to hold a meeting outside, in the Square. The police intervened. They got themselves all taken to the police station: as the rooms were big enough, they were able at last to have their meeting. Ten minutes later the policemen were also taking part in the discussion, which went on into the small hours. Then everyone went home.

I had an astonishing experience, one day when I had come to the Exhibition to give a few technical explanations to some people who were interested. There was a considerable crowd, as there was every day. The great revelation of the Exhibition was Georges Braque. After last year's storm over Picasso the iconoclast, the Muscovites found Braque reassuring, almost classic, the master of a beauty that was, in a word, eminently assimilable. They themselves were quite surprised by it. I too was surprised by this unanimity: workers unpacking the cases became transfixed in front of 'The Yellow Lemons'; painters at the private view and students from the Beaux-Arts, who killed me with questions one evening, all were repeating: 'Braque. . . . Ah, Braque! . . . Talk to us about Braque. . . .' And that is what, on the day in question, thirty or forty young people said to me as they surrounded me, when they heard me speaking French and guessed who I was. They were a group of students from a school for teachers. I had practically to give a lecture. There was a run of questions about Braque, about Picasso, about abstract painting. One boy asked me: 'Would M. Vercors tell us what he thinks of Soviet painting?' I was given neither the time nor the trouble of answering: a great roar of laughter greeted the question. So much so that, in order not to look as if I had come in a destructive spirit, it was I who attempted, with a smile, a defence. Oh! it was only a sketch, but even that was too much. 'Perhaps,' I hazarded, 'in certain social conditions these topical works may also justify their existence. . . .' 'But not so many!' shouted one of them, again in the midst of laughter. I thought of those young people when, a few days later, I found myself face to face with some twenty pupils of the Surikov Institute of Painting. For that was pathetic. It is easier for students of mechanics or of education to throw overboard thirty years of bad painting than it is for young painters who are preparing to take over. They were trying to understand everything, but as they understood they felt the ground giving under their feet. And so they clung to the branches. I shook, they let go, they clung again. And yet it was not they who had had enough at midnight, but I.

I may seem to have strayed, to be rather forgetting the main thing, in favour of a secondary field. This is not unintentional. What is happening in the field of painting is in the image of what is happening or beginning to happen in the other fields. If at any moment I had been afraid that, by going to Moscow, I might have made a blunder (as the French Embassy tried, I think, to give me to understand, by not replying, even with

a word, to my card and by almost completely ignoring the
Exhibition), I should have been reassured by all the gratitude
which so many people over there showed me. I found it moving,
it went so far beyond its modest object! I myself had taken so
little trouble, and the thanks were due in the first place to the
publishers. The gratitude was clearly meant for the support
contributed to a field far vaster than the organization of an
exhibition. I should like to relate a very small but moving and
significant incident. While we were unpacking the cases a short
man in his sixties happened to pass through, on some business.
He was a painter, he could speak French a little, and he went
from one picture to another, repeating ceaselessly, with staring
eyes: 'What wealth! What wealth! . . .' He told us that he had
spent two or three years in Paris, had known Soutine and
Chagall, and had worked with them. Obviously he was one of
the painters who had been kept out of things during all these
years because of their non-conformism, and who were only
just beginning to come back to the surface again. We saw him
again, a few days later, visiting the Exhibition with his wife.
Farther on, a group of young people was going from one picture
to another, arguing with passionate fervour in front of Braques
and Picassos and Modiglianis. As one of them seemed to us to
be rather dominating the controversy, we asked our painter to
go and listen and tell us what he was saying. His wife remained
with us. A minute later we saw that none of them was speaking
any more: it was our old painter who was talking, surrounded
by a respectful audience. . . . Somebody came up to us and
whispered: 'Who is speaking?' The old painter's wife turned
round, with a contained but radiant expression on her face. As
though she had been touched at last, after long hours of night,
by the light from a distant star – a star whose light had taken
thirty years to reach her: 'It's the painter Novgorod,' she said. She
said it with a gravity so proud and happy, that to have given her
that minute would have been enough to repay me for my trouble.

.   .   .   .   .

I have shown – I fear at some length – why I did not, in
fact, leave 'empty-hearted'. My hands, as I have made clear,

are less full. It would be unjust, however, to give the appearance of admitting that they received nothing. Practically, the objective I had set myself was not to convince anyone but to obtain a meeting of the writers of our three countries, Hungary, France and the Soviet Union. I rather quickly realized that I could, by forcing things, obtain a tripartite meeting, but that it would not be very profitable, and might even be more harmful than useful; that, on the contrary, meetings two by two, beginning with the Hungarians and Soviets, followed by the Hungarians and the French, the French and the Soviets, would be more free and would bear better fruit. It is not for me to vaunt here the resistance I had to overcome. Let it suffice that, when I left Moscow, this suggestion was generally accepted; an eminent member of the Union was to leave for Budapest to make the first contacts. To be perfectly frank, I was assured that I would receive prompt news, and I have not received it yet. I can merely say that I hope to have it soon.

I was also promised that if we wrote again – I or others – to the Soviet writers letters in the same spirit as those which received no reply, they would be published and reply would be made. I recall that the silence of the writers came from their disagreement, and from their reluctance to let it transpire. The promise made to me is therefore not without value – if, of course, it is kept.

It will be seen that, without minimizing these results, I bring back more hope in my heart than in my hands. I was more than once moved, sometimes even overwhelmed, by so many agonized efforts to find the right way; more than once, as I saw those poets and painters emerging from the night, and those young people discovering a world, I thought: 'We must, we *must*, help them!' It would be idiotic, if not criminal, to help against them, by our incomprehension or resentment, the die-hards and profiteers of the régime, to whom any tragic accident like Hungary is opportunity for strengthening themselves in their thousands of Bastilles: 'Just look where your follies lead us!' I speak, of course, as a man loyal to the spirit of the Socialist Revolution, which, in spite of its past errors and crimes, remains in my eyes the hope of a thousand million human beings. As a man who works as best he can to make it recover its purity, who suffers when it lapses, and rejoices when it returns. For those who see no other hope than its pure and simple destruction, all that I have just said is clearly of no importance.

. . . . .

While some readers, after the publication of this article, signified to me their approval, I had not the same luck with all. Some thought me too indulgent, others too reserved. Among the very people I thought I was serving (the Soviet writers) some reproached me for what I had said. My 'we must help them' wounded them: 'We need help from no one.' It is true I ought rather to have written 'support them'. It was conveyed to me also that, to speak of 'clandestine poets' was incorrect, and it is true that I should have written: 'authors of poems not published but circulating from hand to hand'. A friend over there, a woman, the one who had said to me: 'Do you realize what it means to lose one's ideal?' wrote to assure me that she had not lost her bearings as much as that. In short, I had some reason to be uncertain that I had done a good job.

There remained the promise, thanks to which I hoped that I had not come home 'empty-handed'. When, more than three months later, the Hungarian writer Gali and the journalist Obersovsky had their prison sentence commuted to the death penalty, I was still without news. I telegraphed to my friends Surkov and Polevoi, secretaries of the Union of Soviet Writers:

Seeing renewal of terror against Hungarian intellectuals remind you your promise and beg you for honour of Socialism join your efforts with those of Picasso, Sartre, Tzara, Montand, etc., to avoid fresh injustices as at time of Babel and other writers now rehabilitated.

V.

I received no reply. It is not impossible that they did none the less intervene, although the inverse commutation of the sentence – from death to prison – arrived too soon to encourage that hope. However that may be, I received some time afterwards a (very friendly) letter from the writer who, as I had been promised, was to go to Budapest to make the first contact with his colleagues. He informed me that the journey had not taken place, because circumstances had not been favourable. He did not explain what circumstances, and seemed not to expect that the journey was postponed to a later date.

Thus the answer came, after four months: I had, in the last resort, come back empty-handed.

.   .   .   .   .

The conclusions will appear gloomy, even if the 'testament' is not.

'*Must we mourn the loss of a great hope?*' I had asked in my letter to the Soviet writers.

In so far as that hope rested on them, we shall have, I fear, to resign ourselves. We shall not obtain from them what we desired. Friendship, yes. That depth of soul and warmth of heart that attracted us in the characters of so many Russian novels will always be found in them, as I found them; and from this point of view, what most of us can offer them in return will always appear skimped and mean. There are many fields in which we shall still be their debtors, and in which they will still have much more to give us than we shall be able to return.

But that especial hope – the one which we harboured for several months, that of debating together some of the great problems of our time – that of watching together over the destinies of Socialism – that of together redressing the errors of Socialism – I am afraid that, as far as I am concerned, I shall have to give it up. While I am sure that, in private, we shall go on with this major dialogue with a few of them who are stauncher or bolder than the rest, we shall not establish it with the others, and we shall not carry it, with them, before the principal interested party, public opinion. It may be that they cannot, it may be that twenty years of contrary habits have made them unlearn independence as we conceive it. They will not break the mould.

Should we therefore throw the helve after the hatchet?

I answer, no less firmly: No. And here, on this point, is my concluding song:

The Lay, or Bequests, of Bruller, alias Vercors

Now I bequeath to youth – the best,
scientists, painters and the rest –
the things the writers will let lie.

They'll pick 'em up (certain am I
of that) and not need to be pressed.
As for the writers, they will talk
within neat limits, neatly dressed,
will hope, swop wounds where'er they walk,

and cultivate torment and doubt:
decide, though? Never! trail about
when it's for them to give the lead.
But there, no help for that; they're through:
from always being the ones to cede
they'll do what they are told to do.
Yet horn and die are there at need:
youth will go on from deed to deed.

So I desire, to these upstarts,
the world's youth who in Moscow wear
the glad hopes of Earth's hundred shores
around their necks or in their hair,
to leave this legacy: the heart's
message and – still more – reason's light.
Against the Devil and his arts
you'll be all right, being in the right.

. . . .

Next to my French friends here and now
I would bequeath all that I know
and all that year by year I learn:
Often history circles round;
to say 'I'm through!' is never sound,
better to wait at the next turn:
talk it out, look ahead, astern,
give and take, and as you pay earn.

Then to the young I spoke of – you
Soviet ones, and others too –
I leave this charge to execute:
Hold on to what you've understood.
You've learned much more than many would
and shown yourselves shrewd and acute.

Remember, catchpennies get caught;
hold your 'no compromise!' – it's good.

To all the clap-trap without end
be deaf – it serves but to corrupt.
The truth! that is your real friend.
Lies can give you no bite or sup:
turn carrion, scarce fit to cut up.
Truth – don't forget – the truth, the total
truth, nothing but. Then – *allez-up!* –
your springs to summer prove their title.
                              Amen.

3

Powerful I am and have no Force or Power

OR THE PILGRIM WITHOUT A STAFF

IT is mainly within the Peace Movement that I have fulfilled for many years the difficult function of *potiche d'honneur*. It would be churlish of me to complain of this, expecially here. This employment has brought me many satisfactions, and most profitable ones: thanks to it I have got to know China and travelled to various places where I could feed on experiences rich in human interest.

Nor do I repudiate the words which, in that capacity, I was called upon to pronounce on great occasions. The most significant of these will be found on the following pages. It is true also that I sometimes played a less verbal part: at Helsinki, during a whole day and the whole of the following night, I helped to suspend the rupture between the Peace Movements of the Arab countries and of Israel and, for the time being, to prevent it. And the fact that I was chosen to make the customary speech when the Peace Prize was given to President Herriot was due to my having been, perhaps, the warmest partisan – and artisan – of that choice. But these, together with a few other occasions of various kinds, were only exceptions. On the whole I merely carried out modestly my decorative function.

After the Budapest insurrection this simple rôle became difficult. Today I consider it impossible, at least for the time being.

My loyalty to the movement had, in my view, one single necessary and sufficient reason: to prevent, by means of the presence in its ranks of many 'liberals' of my kind, the Peace Movement from yielding to the excessive weight which was bearing it down to one side. Helsinki seemed to mark the success of our hopes: I am sure, even today, that the movement had won by its perseverance the confidence of all those men or organizations for whom peace is the supreme good. The Hungarian tragedy threw the movement back into its old ruts (I am thinking here of the French section) – those of Communist intransigence and, in case of serious divergence, its complete dominance. At the last National Council it was still possible to believe that not all was decided. Perhaps indeed not all is, even yet; but at it I had explained very clearly what guarantees a *potiche d'honneur* like me would have to be given, and I was not granted them. I must, therefore, 'wait and see', as they say, before returning to my display shelf in the French section of the Movement.

A DAY WITH CHARLIE CHAPLIN

It was in June that I went to deliver the Peace Prize to Charlie Chaplin: perhaps a little over four months ago. Usually such meetings leave little impression on my overloaded memory: in the last few years I have seen too many things and too many people to retain much that is worth while. Everything slips between my fingers and I count myself lucky if I remember the essential point of a discussion, the expression on someone's face, or sometimes a phrase that has struck me.

But if I were to try to describe that day with Charlie Chaplin, hours would not be enough: I can remember it all. It is with the man as with his films. What other films could I recount from end to end without forgetting a single image, as I can *Happy Times*, which I saw more than thirty years ago, unless it be *The Kid*, *Shoulder Arms*, *The Pilgrim*, *City Lights*, and all the others? The phenomenon is really unique and fantastic. I have forgotten so many things out of my own life, but from the life of that little fellow with the huge feet I have mislaid nothing.

I could today relate that bright day with him minute by minute. I will try to confine myself and tell only the main things.

I thought I was going to see a man difficult of access, somewhat gloomy and rather silent. I found a laughing, affable man, anxious to please and more talkative than anyone. I am always scared of having to keep up conversation, especially with someone I admire. My fears were indeed superfluous. All I had to do was to shut my mouth and listen. All we had to do – there were five of us present – was to listen in silence. Chaplin did all the work. It is as if he could not bear the slightest silence, as though he accused himself of negligence: as if it were his social duty that his guests should not for a moment cease laughing and being amused. And I must say, we did not, for a moment.

In all this verbal agitation there is not the slightest 'side'. Quite the contrary – it seems rather to be the after effect of an old uneasiness, impossible to uproot. Thirty-five years ago fame descended on him, and for thirty-five years he has never managed altogether to believe in it. But since he has got to believe in it, he keeps asking himself what would have happened to him if glory had remained aloof. What he most admires – he told us this, and one could feel that it came from his deepest self – is the man who continues to believe in himself in spite of the world's incomprehension. Who continues to hold fast to his own ideas in face of all that indifference. Like Van Gogh, like Edgar Allen Poe. He himself remembers his astonishment when, thinking he had utterly failed in Hollywood, he took the train for New York after having telegraphed his brother to look for a job for him. The telegraphist had passed the news all down the line. And at every station there was a delirious crowd to welcome him. That is how he learned that he was famous. He 'could not get over it'. He has still not altogether 'got over it'.

'If you happen to have seen a film of mine called *The Gold Rush* . . .' he said to us in connexion with a shack in his garden. And that was no affectation. He was always surprised, absolutely enchanted, when one of us mentioned one of his old films. 'Is that so? Have you seen it?' And he would immediately act the scene in question all over again. You can imagine the feast it was for us! We spoke of those politicians who by their folly led men to ruin; 'And men let them,' said Chaplin sadly;

'Why don't they send them packing?' 'It's like,' I said to him, 'in your film, *Charlie the Watchmaker*: people cannot believe that the "specialist" sometimes knows less about it than the man in the street. So the man in the street lets him hack his alarm clock to pieces before his eyes with a tin opener, spread its innards all over the table, lose the half of them and shove the rest back higgledy-piggledy into the case, and dares not say a word. "He knows better than I do," he thinks; even when the clockmaker gives his alarm clock back to him with an air of disgust. . . .' 'Yes!' exclaimed Chaplin, and aughed and enjoyed the joke as if it was somebody else's, and held the clock out to us with an air of powerlessness and disgust – with such marvellous mimicry that we roared with laughter, and he most of all.

And he was pleased because he has not yet (after thirty-five years) got used to people asking his opinion, or, above all, to taking it seriously: after all, perhaps his is as good as that of the 'specialist's'? It was a constant delight to him.

What parts did he not play before us in a few hours! The whole of America in one scene in a drug-store: a simple scene in which all the boredom and ill humour of a society built on absurd foundations break out in a simple conversation between a customer asking for hamburgers and a waiter who has no hamburgers. An endless scene, with a monotony so mercilessly sad and dull that it made one shudder as much as it made one laugh. 'While here,' Chaplin exclaimed, 'people like eating, and they like living!'

All the vulgarity of the American ruling class in a single word when, at the request of one of the Press magnates, he had invited this excessively prominent man to a meal with Einstein. But the two could not think of a single word to say to each other. The silence became unbearable. Then the disastrous 'star' – a female whom the terrible potentate was then imposing on the public by dint of dollars, suddenly turned towards the old scientist, who sat next to her, and, wriggling her fingers over his leonine mane. 'When,' she cried, with a nasal twang (Chaplin imitating that twang!) 'when are you going to get a hair-cut?'

All the Chinese (and Japanese) theatre, with all its colour and truculence, the din of the orchestra's gongs and cymbals, the shrill singing of the heroine, her death, the rose petals thrown over her with an exquisite gesture, the *décors*, the scene shifters. . . . How many arms and hands, instruments and vocal chords, I asked myself, has this diabolical man at his disposal? And I myself fell into the trap: he was telling my wife, in an English that was too quick for me, a story interspersed with long bits of Chinese. 'He knows Chinese as well!' I thought, marvelling. But that was just the point of the story: when he got back from the Far East, where he had spent six weeks about fifteen years ago, Douglas Fairbanks had invited him to dinner, saying with a laugh: 'You will be able to chatter away in Chinese with my boy.' Chaplin arrived, the boy was sent for, and they started an endless conversation. The guests were flabbergasted and wide-eyed: to have learned Chinese like that in six weeks! This went on till Chaplin suddenly hesitated over a word: 'How . . . how do you say inscrutable in Chinese?' It was only then that they understood that Chaplin was playing a trick on them and had got the boy to enter into the game: but they had not managed to distinguish between Chaplin's Chinese and that of the boy. . . .

What else could I not tell? Alas, we must draw the line somewhere. Why not conclude with the answer he gave, in our presence, to an importunate journalist? The whole of Chaplin's 'committed art', to use the current phrase, is contained in the humour of that reply. The journalist was insidiously trying to make him say more than he wished about his next film. 'It will be funny,' Chaplin kept saying, obstinately. 'People were rather hoping,' the journalist said, with a deceptively innocent smile, 'that you would have a go at McCarthy and his crowd.' 'No, no,' said Chaplin, 'fleeting things like that, you know. . . . My film will be funny, that's all.' 'Can I say, then,' the journalist insisted, 'that your new film will be entirely non-political?' 'N-no,' said Chaplin, with a slight grimace, 'you can't say that either.'

And while the journalist was scratching his head, he repeated: 'Say that I hope it will make people laugh. That's all.'

Yes: laugh, with that vengeful laugh that shook me yesterday evening as I saw, yet again, *Modern Times*, which has not aged by a single wrinkle. The same warm laugh that shakes the young of today, severe and difficult though they are, as it did those twenty years ago (the young painter who is working with me on my *'callichromies'* has seen the film twice running and intends to go again – he does not want to lose a single detail). The laughter with which Chaplin himself gently stressed that little phrase he had slipped *en passant* into his statement on the Peace Prize he had just received: 'because all nations, great and small, will soon be able to have the H-bomb . . .' – and he emphasized the word 'small': 'That will give 'em a jolt,' he said, 'the idea that even the small nations. . . .' And the man who, in all his films, has shown us poor little Charlie, puny and luckless, triumphing in the end, every time, over the bully who thinks he can do what he likes, rubbed his hands.

(1954)

SPEECH ON HANDING THE PEACE PRIZE TO CHARLES CHAPLIN

In the name of the World Peace Council and of the members of the International Peace Prize jury, I have the signal honour to hand you the laureate's diploma which has been accorded to you.

It is not only an honour for me to have been appointed to hand it to you, it is also a very great joy. For not far short of forty years I have loved and admired you as a man of peace – perhaps you are the first man who made me understand the criminal stupidity of war. I was a child at the time of the First World War. And the war appeared to me as a glorious adventure, which excited my childish imagination all the more because it was not I who was called upon to pay the price of that glory or the sufferings of that adventure, but men unknown to me, sunk in fear and mud. And then, one fine day, when the guns were still thundering, an extraordinary film tore to shreds, by the extraordinary power of laughter, the bloodstained banners of military glory. Ever since that day I have seen war as you showed it to us: an ignoble crushing of man, disguised hypocritically beneath a glory invented by the mystifiers.

For forty years since then you have stubbornly shown us what man really is: a tiny light crushed beneath the blind powers of nature and deriving his only dignity, his only great-ness, from refusing to submit to these as an animal does, and from picking himself up after every defeat – even if he is fore-doomed to be beaten – to carry on once more an endless struggle. And those who, instead of helping him, take sides with the executioner to gain advantage from his defeat – you have shown us how blind and foolish they themselves are, since they do not see that the executioner already has his axe poised above their own heads. Thus for forty years you have been showing us that there is no other reasonable course for all men than that of peace, than that of their fraternal alliance against those blind powers, in an atmosphere of mutual love and help.

That is why, having myself tried to follow in your footsteps and to show in my books what you have shown in such masterly fashion in your films, I feel it is a wonderful recompense for my own efforts that I should be the one who today places this diploma in your hands.

(1954)

SPEECH ON HANDING THE PEACE PRIZE TO PROFESSOR DE CASTRO

The great advances of mankind have always been made in the same way: calling in question what seemed established for ever. This is a mental exertion requiring a by no means common strength of character. Nothing, in fact, is more contrary to the nature of mind than to cast doubt on what it knows, or on what it thinks it knows. Those who thus dare to make a clean slate of all the things they know in order to examine them afresh are called Pasteur or Einstein, Michurin or de Castro.

It required your penetration and your patience, Monsieur le Président, to establish – against the stream of ideas so wide-spread that they appeared unquestionable – the fundamental error of the theories of Malthus and of Vogt. To show that the

hunger of great masses of human beings like those of Brazil or
India is not a natural phenomenon, an inevitable calamity,
a scourge against which men can do little; to show us, with
startling clarity, that, far from poverty being a consequence of
over-population, it is on the contrary over-population that is
a consequence of poverty. That it is through a just distribution
of consumer goods that the balance between the earth and the
men who inhabit it will be established, without need for those
barbarous means which were supposed to be the only ones
capable of achieving it – the pacific expedient of birth-control
and the violent and criminal method of wars of extermination.
Already, of course, we felt a whole-hearted indignation when
confronted with such cynical theories, the theories of people
who claimed to be realists and said that one should be glad at
heart that there are earthquakes, cholera, years of drought,
Yellow River floods and also – between ourselves, of course – a
few massacres here and there like those of Warsaw or Hiroshima,
because just imagine what the population of this small planet
would be without those famines, epidemics and slaughters. . . .
Yes, certainly we were furiously indignant, but sometimes we
were at a loss for a reply to these appalling sophisms. And then
you came, Monsieur le Président, bringing us more arguments
than we had dared to hope for. You showed us that these
sophisms are not merely profoundly ignoble but quite simply
blind and foolish. You showed us that the earth contains within
it wealth enough of all kinds to feed so many more people than
its present population, that the whole planet is still at the stage
of resembling the Europe of the tenth century – a Europe
traversed by cruel famines even though its entire population at
that time was less than that of Switzerland or Holland today.
You showed us that poverty makes families too large and well-
being diminishes them. You have shown us an enormous
number of other fascinating and marvellous things, which have
nourished in us our trust in mankind and the hopes we place
in its destiny. In thus demonstrating the mistakenness of the
man-eaters, the mistakenness of those who claim to fight against
hunger by the suppression of the hungry; in demonstrating that,
on the contrary, this immemorial scourge will be wiped from

the surface of the globe by means of the pacific organization of food production and distribution, by the suppression of colonialism and its methods (as barbarous and primitive now as in the time of Chilperic), and by ending the armaments race which enriches ten men and ruins ten millions: you have contributed not only to the cause of reason, not only to that of justice, but also to that of Peace, and so you have nobly deserved, on top of so many other distinctions which have already proclaimed the value of your work and of your efforts, this International Peace Prize which I have the honour and the very great pleasure of handing to you here.

(1955)

SPEECH ON THE MOSCOW RADIO

The World Assembly at Helsinki set before itself a definite aim: at the moment when there is hope of a world political *détente*, at the moment when the heads of the great powers are on the point of meeting at Geneva, to unite in an expression of common purpose all the forces of peace, all the organizations or personalities that are fighting for the victory of peace, whatever their opinions or tendencies.

Has the World Assembly succeeded in this ambitious design? It would have been Utopian to hope for it to do so completely. At the heart of the various forces whose only common ideal, still, is peace, there remain too many divergencies, too many contradictions, for it to be possible for these to disappear so quickly. Many organizations and many people one would like to see at Helsinki did not think fit to be present at the Assembly. But many of those that did not venture either to Warsaw or to Vienna overcame their scruples this time and took part in our work. This is a considerable encouragement. They included men whose credit with the absent is great enough to win them over, to bring those hesitant ones nearer to us. First and foremost, this credit will have the effect of breaking down the barrier of suspicion with which the propaganda of our adversaries surrounded us. Already certain individuals with a world-wide authority, such as Queen Elizabeth of Belgium or President

Herriot, and others who formerly were often against our movement, such as the British philosopher, Bertrand Russell, or the
Reverend Candy, have come into the open and proclaimed
their support for us before all the world. Many Western
journalists who were at Helsinki, and who had begun their
reports in a tone of more or less malevolent scepticism, were
later forced to change the colour of their ink and to admit the
vigour and sincerity of the Assembly's work and the exemplary
value of the agreements reached in the committees. It is too
soon to foresee what influence these various victories will have
upon the work of the four heads of States. It is in any case hard
to believe they will have none. For some years now we have
realized that public opinion is no longer a negligible force. It
has stopped two wars – in Korea and in Indo-China. It has
several times prevented an international war from breaking out
and the nuclear bomb from being used. The will of the peoples
to live in peace, as now made clear at Helsinki on an even
larger scale than before, will be heard at Geneva, even if some
people pretend to be unwilling to listen to it.

(1955)

FINAL INTERVENTION[1] (Extracts)

... When something grave happens, our rôle is not that of
a tribunal, it is not for us to justify or condemn, but we do have
to say – and we cannot escape from this rôle – whether the event
in question is or is not a danger to peace, whether it is or is not
already a step into war.

Sometimes the answer is so obvious that it raises no problem
among us. Such was the case with Suez and Algeria. But at
other times it is much less obvious, and then the event does not
call forth the same answer from all of us, because it provokes
different interpretations. My last allusion here to the Hungarian
affair will be to say that it has just shown us in a striking manner
what happens among us in such cases.

I will remind you of a story which you probably know. The
story of the energetic husband who made a treaty with his wife

[1] In the National Council on 2 December 1956.

about authority. 'When we agree,' he said, 'we do what I decide. When we disagree, we do what she decides.' In that way, he explained, there was never a quarrel in the household. . . .

That is to some extent an image of what happens here, in the Peace Movement, and there is no need for me to illustrate how things go when we are not all of the same opinion about the interpretation of an event.

. . . A writer . . . certainly represents a certain audience which is part of public opinion – at least as long as it still has some confidence in him. But what he does directly, from the point of view of action, is obviously rather slight. The fact remains that, in spite of that, a good many of these personalities are members of the bureau of the National Council. This probably means that their figuring there has not been judged useless. And perhaps they did in fact help our recent delegation to Helsinki, and even the other delegations. But if they are useful there, then life must not be made impossible for them.

The family I mentioned just now is a model family as long as husband and wife are of the same opinion. That was the case with us for a long time. But when they cease to be so, and when the poor husband has no longer the right to think anything but what his wife thinks, he may stand for it once or twice – at least in small matters – but if a serious difficulty arises, he will end by raising hell. Especially when he sees that he has lost all his authority, not only in his own household but even with the few friends who had remained loyal to him.

You understand: take me, for instance; I am content to be a *potiche d'honneur* for the Peace Movement. Even if, when we have a different opinion from our Communist friends, all we are allowed to do is to pocket it and stuff a handkerchief on top. I am content to stay, none the less, if wanted, but I can no longer very well understand what can be the use of a series of *potiches* that are now only cracked ones. . . .

I am asking you the question, that is all. It is for you to decide what you want. To decide if it is enough for you that we should be this flea-market junk, or if, on the contrary, you want us to hold our place in the struggle. But we can only hold our place if we stop being like the poor husband I spoke of. . . .

When a grave disagreement comes up, a fraction of the bureau must no longer possess a *de facto* veto which, actually, deprives the other members of the right to take any decision, even if they represent a large majority in the bureau. . . . A majority decision, whatever this majority may be, must be transmitted to the federations. The minority will still have the right to make its different point of view known, and the federations the right to take, in their turn, the decision they think fit. But at least any majority decision must be presented to the various peace committees as a recommendation which it is for them to study and discuss.

It seems to me, after the experience of the Hungarian affair, that if we do not in the future adopt a rule of this kind in the functioning of the National Council and its bureau – well, at the next difficulty, whether it arises in connexion with Syria or Israel or any other incident, our bureau will find itself surrounded by a fine heap of broken *potiches*, whose pieces will be past sticking together again. And as we consider that there is no point in finding ourselves in such a situation, which can do no good to anyone, some of us will have to resign ourselves to continuing the struggle for peace in a more modest rank. That, I repeat, no longer depends on us, but on you. . . .

.   .   .   .   .

That is how things stand.

The bureau's decisions continue, as before, to obey the rule of unanimity – which means that the majority has in fact to bow to the veto of the minority. For eight years husband and wife were agreed on the essential, and this led to no trouble. For the last year it has no longer, unfortunately, been so. It is no longer possible to accept in advance these unilateral decisions.

If, I repeat, I had the time and the temperament to take an active part in the struggles of the Movement, I would fight inside it patiently, to make my point of view prevail. I have not, and I must leave this struggle to others. I hope they will succeed. The tasks of the Movement remain in my view the most urgent ones of our time. The nuclear peril now makes the smallest conflct in the most remote part of the world into a terrible menace to the existence of man on earth. I am still, with all my heart, a friend and ally of those who stubbornly oppose such a peril with the tenacious obstacle of their will, based on the will of the people. Only, I think my name, for the moment, has lost all value for their cause: it is not what holds the loyal ones, and as for the hesitant or the estranged, it has lost currency and repels more of them than it attracts. And so, even to serve peace, the best thing is to temper it afresh for a time in silence. Perhaps after such a cure it will one day be able to serve again a useful purpose.

Does that mean that I have reached the stage of throwing the helve after the hatchet? I answer firmly No!

J

4

Have my own likes, and every Law has me

OR THE SPRINGS OF TILPHUSE

W AS it necessary, or useful, or timely – in a word, was it desirable – to publish the following pages? They are, in fact, for the most part made up of personal letters, sent privately. If in spite of this I have decided to include them, it is because they too form a significant *dossier* – the *dossier* of their own almost complete lack of success, whose constancy it has seemed to me necessary to demonstrate; for while this constant failure makes plain, as far as I myself am concerned, the melancholy decision to retire for some time, it makes no less plain, beyond my person, the deeper meaning behind these failures.

First, a failure in the struggle against forgetfulness: in this last chapter will be found – as already in all my earlier collected essays – some pages that are stubbornly against forgetfulness. Since they were written, we have seen the French Army placed under the orders of a *ci-devant* Hitlerian general; Resistance ministers placing the *ci-devant* Vichy police back in the saddle against their comrades in the Resistance; another resistant proclaiming to all who care to hear that he takes the essence of his policy from a *ci-devant* excellency not long ago condemned to death for treason; another resistant, remaining obstinately deaf to the cries of tortured men, whom he delivered into the 'efficient' hands of a Legion largely recruited from among the former Nazis. And we have just heard an outburst of those songs and yells of sinister memory, chanted beyond the Rhine by several divisions of the S.S. celebrating the memory of their exploits under the indifferent gaze of the world. . . .

Also a failure in the struggle against the rebirth of a German army: on this subject will be found some ten letters 'to various eminent persons'. They were written in alarm, the alarm one feels before a house on fire,

Lez ung brasier frissonnant tout ardent

when your only means of saving it is a telephone and, anyway, nobody answers. Sometimes, as one rereads them, the alarm now seems less understandable, and that is precisely the most alarming thing about them: for here again, once more, forgetfulness has descended, or is descending, on these follies committed against our country, follies we had not the skill, or not the power, to oppose – simply because after a few months the consequences were once again suspended and have not all stricken France yet.

There will also be found here two letters which I wrote to General de Gaulle after the publication of *The Call to Honour*. It is perhaps not without interest, at the moment when his name is being mentioned on various sides with a view to a settlement of the Algerian tragedy, to recall the terms which I considered indispensable eighteen months ago, if such recourse were had to him: working-class backing. To rely on that and save all, or on its adversaries and lose all – is the only choice open to anyone.[1]

The final pages are dominated by the unending tragedy which ravages Algeria, and of which the issue is both desired and feared by every Frenchman, since for France to be driven out of Algeria would be an immense disaster, but to enchain Algeria – for how long? – by means of injustice, flames and bloodshed would be a no less fatal disgrace. The fact that we have been unable, over all these years, in spite of our arguments and appeals, to prevent the accumulated errors, which have brought France where she is, is evidence of the painful powerlessness of the intelligentsia to influence the destinies of the country. Must they simply recognize this powerlessness and fall

---

[1] This was written in the summer of 1957, and published in the autumn of that year – about a year, then, before the present developments in French politics. The terms on which, it is suggested here, a recourse to General de Gaulle could hope to produce favourable consequences, have scarcely been fulfilled.

silent, as I am deciding to do? No, no; I am not falling silent
from discouragement. Mine is a provisional silence, to get my
breath and recover strength. Thus, later on, this voice of goodwill may get a better hearing. For I do not forget – I shall never
forget – the lesson given us, all his life long, by one of the great
dead, the lesson of Romain Rolland.

THE MAN WHO NEVER WEAKENED [1]

'What I most admire' – Charlie Chaplin said to me when
I went to give him the Peace Prize – 'what I most admire is not
so much any successful man. On the contrary, it is the man who
has everyone against him, and who goes on, all the same, along
the road he has chosen, because in spite of this hostility (or
indifference) he has too much spirit to let himself be influenced,
or to lose faith in himself and in the rightness of his cause.'

He said that to me on the heights which dominate the Lake
of Geneva, and how could I avoid, as I listened to him, thinking
of another hill, that neighbouring hill at Villeneuve, where
Romain Rolland lived for so long, and against which the waves
of incomprehension beat for so many years?

I was very young then, a child, and I lived in an environ-
ment of patriotic *bourgeois*, some of whom came from Alsace,
driven out from there by Prussia; and the anger they felt
against Romain Rolland – how could I have helped sharing it?
Like the war this anger seemed to me just and sacred. Even
when, as I grew older and began to think, I began to doubt that
right was on one side only, I still persisted in telling myself that,
if perhaps France was not entirely right, Romain Rolland had
none the less let her down. His stubbornness seemed to me
diabolic. It took years more, long reflection and laborious
analysis before I was able to understand that it was, on the
contrary, Romain Rolland who had long been the only – or
in any case the first – guardian of the honour of France. The
admiration I came to feel then for this clear-sightedness, this
determination, this perseverance and incredible courage, has
never declined since. For the last quarter of a century the

[1] For the tenth anniversay of the death of Romain Rolland (1955).

example of Romain Rolland has been, for me as for many others, the immutable lighthouse on its rock resisting the surge, the flow and ebb and every attack from tempest or thunderstorm. When lassitude comes, with the temptation to weaken, to let go of the heavy oars and yield feebly to the current, one has only to raise one's eyes: the lighthouse is there, the man who never weakened. His light still illuminates sky and sea, and one would feel too much of a coward if one gave up. And so the name of Romain Rolland is to us like those talismans which the primitive warriors used furtively to touch, to make sure of being brave in battle: we evoke it, and we feel assured against ourselves, make our flight impossible for ourselves, prop ourselves against him as though with our backs to the wall. For my part, this supreme comfort has never failed me.

LETTERS TO CERTAIN V.I.P.S[1] (1955)

It is not perhaps usual to publish in book form letters sent privately.

But when the very future of the country, perhaps its life or death, is involved – and perhaps the future of the whole world, its life or death – it seems to me that any example is worth showing, which others may follow in their turn.

Up to the day when I wrote the first letter published here, I had never privately approached influential persons in the hope of influencing them. This must have been because I did not believe in it, did not believe that the daily life of politics could leave those who give their energies to it the time to pay attention, among the innumerable correspondence they receive, to the letter of a man they do not know, except in some cases by reputation.

It was alarm that suddenly made me decide to do so. Sick and exhausted, I was unable to take part in the collective activities for peace, against German rearmament. I could not bear this inaction. That is why I wrote the first letters. Then, once having got under way, just

---

[1] These pages were collected together once before, in the hope of bringing them out as a pamphlet before the Paris Agreements (on German rearmament) were voted. But the time was too short for this, and the author abandoned a publication which would in consequence have been too late – or too early. They are published now, without cuts or changes, for the sake of the thoughts they may suggest at this distance.

before the December vote in the Assembly, to attempt a personal approach to the deputies who were in favour of the Paris Agreements. I drafted a letter, ran off 400 copies, and sent it to them, in most cases to their private address.

I have no means of measuring the success, or lack of success, of these letters. If a few votes changed at the last moment, how can one know whether this effort in extremis had anything to do with it? I can at least be sure they were read. I received a considerable number of replies. Some of these called forth a fresh reply from me. It is these few letters that form the essential part of this small work, which has no other ambition than to show the reader that his opinion can and must *be expressed with confidence and obstinacy. Never has this necessity been so pressing as in these anxious days.*   *15 March 1955*

Letter to François Mauriac

23 November 1954

Perhaps I am indulging in illusions as to the influence it is possible to have on Pierre Mendès-France – perhaps he listens to no one, not even to you. Also I do not know what you now think of me after so many years, but what can one do when one's mind is overflowing with alarm? The doctor's advice at present forbids me an active life, as the result of a serious setback, otherwise I should be at Stockholm, for the first time since Pleyel in 1949, and should there relieve my anguish in the struggle. I should in any case have gone there in an unhappy mood. The end of my last book shows plainly the hope I shared with so many other people last July. I still think it would be disastrous to overthrow Mendès-France. It is he, therefore, who has to be convinced – but by whom, and how? Are you not frightened, François Mauriac? I know your gaze is fixed rather on Morocco, it was Morocco that enlightened you (in my case it was Indo-China), and it is still your touchstone. But do you realize that the agreements reached in London no longer forbid Germany the atom bomb? She has not yet the right to produce them, but she has already the right to acquire them – this has just emerged in the debates in the House of Commons. Eden

was cornered and admitted it. Do you realize that only yesterday Kesselring was speaking on British television, rehabilitating
the S.S. and vaunting their warlike virtues? The E.D.C.
frightened us because it ill concealed its essential aim: to
paralyse France, since she was too disquieting with her quarter
of Communist voters. What can we do if threatened by a
German atomic bomb – except throw ourselves into the arms
of the Russians? I know: Pierre Mendès-France sincerely wants
negotiation, sincerely counts on it. But suppose it fails? Suppose
America or Russia sabotage it – suppose Germany does? Or
suppose he himself falls in the meantime? What a terrible risk
to run!

Can he still be held back, persuaded not to commit himself
personally to a hasty ratification – at least not to commit himself to any date? The choice is intolerable, either to ratify the
German atomic bomb (and the S.S. generals), or to see the
return of MM. Baylot and Martineau-Deplat – and *also*, sooner
or later, ratify the bomb and the S.S., unless the country rises in
revolt. Must it be Mendès-France who forces us into this hopeless plight? How one would like to see a man like you still able
to do something! It is not possible that we are already shut up
in this rat-trap, able only to run round and round and strike
against the bars. It is worse when one is bedridden and cannot
even run. That is why I am writing to you. Because one must
try everything, and I cannot bear any longer this anguished
immobility.

Reply to François Mauriac

30 November 1954

Of course the German atomic bomb is only the more or less
unlikely sting of a much vaster hornet's nest. But it is only one
more gamble: let us take a chance that agreement will be
reached on this point. Let us take a chance that wisdom will
prevail in Germany and elsewhere. Let us take a chance that
negotiation will succeed. Let us take a chance that Germany
will not obstruct it. Let us take a chance that she will not abuse
the powers that are being given her. Let us take a chance that
she will keep Bruening and Hindenburg and not give in to

Hitler, that we shall still have Adenauer and avoid Oberlander, let us take a chance that America will remain loyal to us in case of disagreement over the Sarre or Lorraine[1] (or Poland or the Sudeten districts), let us take a chance that she will not give Germany the means of bringing us to heel if we have the audacity to kick. Let us take a chance. . . .

I can understand that some people may be more reasonable than I and not so frightened by this succession of chances taken; I find it less easy to understand that these should be regarded as a 'fatality', formidable but inevitable. (Why inevitable? I am curious to know what de Gaulle will say on this point.) What seems to me hardest of all to understand is that resignation to a mortal danger should be given a hole-and-corner ratification, without parliament or opinion having the time to size up either the volume of the peril or whether it is really inescapable, whether an agreement with the East is really impossible. I am alarmed at seeing Pierre Mendès-France adopt George Bidault's methods, when the latter disclosed to his ministers at the last moment only Britain's bogus agreement to participate in the E.D.C., so as to make them sign without any real examination (perhaps that was the day when he fell from power). That is what makes me tremble, *cher François Mauriac*. That succession of foolhardy chances taken, and that haste to impose them.

Thank you for having listened to me, I should very much like to be able to talk it all over with you when I am quite well again.[2]

Letter to the Representatives of the People

12 December 1954

This is the first time in my life that I am writing to a representative of the people. It took a great hope, and then the fact of this hope, day by day, giving place to uneasiness, anxiety, alarm – and tomorrow perhaps to terror – to make me decide on a step whose chances of being useless I know too well. Can this letter even reach you? And even if it gets as far as you, will

---

[1] Now already a German minister advocates 'the internationalization of Strasburg . . .' (*note added in 1957*).

[2] There was no further reply and I did not meet François Mauriac.

you take the time to read it, and, even if you read it, will the name of the man who signs it act on your mind and stay in your mind? Will you be willing to remind yourself that this voice did for the first time decide to speak out in spite of the same feeling of helplessness – that desperate enterprise was called *The Silence of the Sea* – and its purpose, then already, was to give warning against a mortal temptation: that of trusting in the best of the Germans – because they have never been able to resist the worst ones.

Thirty million deaths were necessary to wrest from Germany its criminal weapons: are we really going to give them back, on the terrifying chance that this time Germany will keep her promises? If the *Président du Conseil* were himself so much at ease, would he have answered that, if she does not keep them, well then, France will fall back on the Franco-Soviet pact? One stands aghast. Does he not remember how a similar calculation worked out once before? When Georges Bonnet, you remember, plotted simultaneously a deal with Ribbentrop against the Soviets and one with Molotov against Germany, he had not thought of this quite simple thing, that the Russians were neither at his orders nor fools, and that he was leaving them only a third way out – that of turning the tables on him and coming to an understanding with Ribbentrop at our expense. If they do the same again tomorrow, what leg shall we have to stand on?

I remember, from my childhood, a scene in a marionette play: Polichinelle gave Gnafron a stick to beat Guignolet. Whereupon Guignolet offered Gnafron a bag of coins to beat Polichinelle. 'Help, Guignolet!' cried Polichinelle, under his own stick. That made us roar with laughter.

Today I should no longer laugh. 'Between war and shame,' said Churchill to Chamberlain after Munich, 'you have chosen shame and you will get war.' 'You have chosen the Germans out of fear of the Russians, and you will get them both' – I hope this paraphrase may not be a prophecy.

But I cannot do anything to stop it being one, and I feel unbearable alarm at seeing Pierre Mendès-France, in his turn, acting like Polichinelle, like Georges Bonnet. And at seeing the

Assembly ready to follow him. I no longer hope that this letter may yet make you hesitate. But what did I hope in 1941, when I began to write? It is a torment no less grave that moves me now.

Letter to M. de Sesmaisons

20 December 1954

I thank you sincerely for the trouble you have taken to reply to me.

Will you allow me to say that abstention was not your line, nor that of your son, nor my own, at certain moments which I believe to be scarcely more tragic for France than those we are about to go through?

What is now in question is not a break with 'those who were our allies all through the war' (although only Great Britain was *all* through the war, then the U.S.S.R., and *lastly* the U.S.A.), but simply the choice between immediate ratification and ratification at a future date (or even by stages). If you genuinely think that mere hesitation would be more grave for France than the dangers of the German Army, the right thing is to vote *for* immediate ratification. And *against* in the opposite case. But is not abstaining a rather insecure means of not being an accomplice of a crime against France while at the same time letting the others commit it? Forgive me for being so bold as to speak to you like this, but my alarm is great.

Letter to M. Daniel Mayer

15 January 1955

Monsieur,

No, I have not changed any more than you have since, in *The Silence of the Sea*, I struggled, desperately already, against the temptation of a tragic marriage in which France would exchange her independence for a mess of pottage. But, Monsieur, 'all dictatorships'? You know very well it is not as simple as that – it would be too easy for the two of us to throw them in each other's teeth, beginning with that of Franco, whom everybody leaves in peace nowadays, and whom we shall soon be made to accept as an ally. My one anxiety, my one worry, is still France – I shall honestly rejoice, believe me, if the future proves you right, if in five years' time Germany has not become once more a dictatorship, more or less disguised. Alas, I foresee on the contrary that the rearmament of Germany means the rebirth of a Germanic grip which will one day be imposed on us: if this is not done by America (as in the case of Guatemala), it will mean that Germany has once again turned to Russia. In either case we should be enslaved before being destroyed.

It is a horrible feeling, seeing this disaster coming so clearly and not being able to stop it. What would I not give if this letter should worry you just for a day, trouble you just for an hour! But it is no doubt useless to hope this.

Letter to M. Daniel Mayer

31 January 1955

Monsieur,

I should deplore it if you were left with a feeling that is unjustified. I do not think I wrote that my letter 'would neither worry nor trouble you' – but almost the opposite: how much would I not give for it to be able to worry and to trouble you. It was an anguished expression of my powerlessness, not an assumption that I was up against a mind devoid of feeling. Why should I have written to you if I had thought that? We are all of us torn in two, I know. But I persist in believing that the worst consequences of a few months' postponement of the ratification of the agreements would have weighed less heavily on my conscience if I had been mistaken than those which, in the contrary case, might one day weigh upon yours? It is this disproportion between the risks that appals me. Rest assured, however, that I shall no less firmly believe in your upright patriotism.

Letter to M. Jules Moch

16 January 1955

Monsieur,

At the risk of seeming importunate I must recur to your reply.

I have naturally never had any doubts of your sincerity or of your freedom of action, as I assume you have no doubts of mine.

I am aware of the good work you have done in the United Nations and I admire it sincerely.

I know that the rearmament of Germany must appear to you in the same light as it does to me, for I have often passed the memorial to your son, by the roadside on the way from Grenoble to the Col de Portes.

But the reasons which have decided you to submit, none the less, to what you recognize to be a 'mistake', only a 'less disastrous one', these reasons seem to me terrifying.

We would be isolated, you say. Our allies would break with us. But, Monsieur, what security is there in such an 'alliance', in which one of the partners can do so well without the other that he threatens a break if he can't have his will? What sort of friend is this, who obliges you to consent to giving their weapons back to your son's murderers, in spite of this repugnance, in spite of this grief? Who will stop him now from rapping us on the knuckles harder still at our slightest move? Ah, Monsieur, believe me, I hope with all my heart – if in the end, Parliament endorses this ratification which two-thirds of public opinion reject – believe me, I hope ardently to see the future prove you right, Russia agree to negotiate, Germany respect the negotiations, and America listen to us instead of bullying us. But frankly I do not believe in it. I believe, alas, that by this submission we shall have lost the authority you were hoping to safeguard, and which only independence, pride and resistance have ever given to a country. I believe, alas, that in a few years the force that will lead Europe will not be ours: it will be Germany's. May Heaven see to it that I am wrong!

Letter to M. Jules Moch

2 February 1955

I am most touched by the trouble you have taken to answer me a second time.

It would be useless to recur to what is done. But what now? I have access to very little political information (but there are situations, like Munich, in which mere common sense is enough), yet it seems to me that one should not throw the helve after the hatchet. What seems to me clear is that we have no longer *a single ally* against a Germany bent on revenge. We have lost the Russians, and we know that in the West we shall be firmly requested to yield on all future points of dispute. Our independence is worth hardly any more than if the E.D.C. had been voted. Is it *really* too late to react? Is it no longer possible, now that we have shown America how far our desire to please her goes, to say to her: 'But no further. Nothing more now before we have talked with the Russians – not even the lodgement of the acts of ratification' (perhaps this is nonsense, for these are juridical tricks of the trade which I do not know)? I cannot conceive that we are without any weapon. We have wasted many cards, but it seems to me that firmness, real firmness, the kind that takes risks, is one which we still have, for a few weeks. After that. . . .

I cannot tell you how deeply uneasy I am, in the real isolation in which we now are, at this pathological need to give way, to submit.

Letter to the Conseillers de la République

10 March 1955

You must have already received so many letters that you are worn out by them. And you have not taken sides in the tragic question of the rearmament of Germany without long moral conflicts. Nor do I wish, therefore, to submit any fresh argument for or against. These arguments have been debated by the National Assembly until often, alas, it could no longer tell head from tail. . . . How many deputies I wonder, in the end abstained because they did not know which danger was the greater – the rebirth of a devouring power at our gates, or the danger, which was being waved before their eyes, of finding ourselves alone?

But your own part, *Monsieur le Sénateur*, though perhaps less burdened by such a choice, is more heavily loaded with a different responsibility: that of seeing more clearly and further. When a problem is drowned in the *imbroglio* of risks and consequences that will never admit of measurement or of justification (since proof by contraries is not possible in History), there remains the supreme recourse: that of choosing justice against injustice.

It was this recourse that saved France, as you know, in the darkest hours of her recent history: when there was no means of foreseeing, after June, 1940, which would win – Germany or England. The Resistance was born of that recourse to Justice over Injustice. It was not the first time, and will not be the last, that it will show the way of salvation. It is thanks to that recourse that France recovered her greatness.

Well, Monsieur, to *whom* are we going to restore weapons?

Are you able to give yourself an answer, to give yourself and the country a clear answer on the following questions?

Is it true, *Monsieur le Sénateur*, that a law voted at Bonn in 1951 guarantees the re-employment of the Nazi officials in all their functions? Is it true that meanwhile they are drawing a provisional pension? That the pension now paid to a certain Rudolf Diel, a former Gestapo chief, is in proportion to the rank he occupied and therefore in proportion to the number of his victims?

Is it true that their victims, on the other hand, if they wish to find employment, must hide the fact that they fought in the German Resistance? That the majority of those who were formerly imprisoned in the concentration camps are having the number, which is tattooed on their arms, effaced by a doubly painful operation, because this number is no longer considered an honour but a disgrace?

Is it true that the widow of one of the most fanatical purveyors of Nazi cemeteries is also drawing a pension proportionate to the judicial rank of her husband, while the widow of a certain democratic deputy, who was tortured and put to death by the men under the orders of that bloodstained procurator, receives less than a tenth of that as compensation?

Is it true that a certain other widow, the widow of a German Jew 'liquidated' in the Riga ghetto from which *not a single* survivor returned, has been refused reparation on the pretext that there is no longer any living witness to 'prove' the death of her husband? That this is only one of a great number of methods used to suspend any compensation to former victims – the most general one being to allot to the examination of their cases so minute a number of officials (and these indeed, most often, former Nazis), that it would take more than twenty years to get through them all? And that thus the majority of the victims will have died meanwhile?

Is it true that, on the other hand, any request for 'reparation' from a former Nazi is immediately considered and granted? That, besides, the German administration as a whole is already, four-fifths of it, in their hands?

Is it true that at least two of Chancellor Adenauer's ministers, Kraft and Oberlander, are former S.S. men of high rank? That one of his closest advisers, Dr. Hans Globke, is the very man who drafted the famous juridical commentaries on Hitler's racial laws – those laws which sent to the ovens more than five million human beings?

These are only a few facts. There are many others. I have chosen these because the newspaper *France-Soir*, which reports them, cannot be suspected of Communist propaganda.

Are they untrue, *Monsieur le Sénateur*?

If you know, if you are sure that they are untrue, you should say so publicly – it will reassure many people's consciences.

If you were unaware of them you should investigate. I have no doubt your own conscience will force you to do so.

And if they are true, and if you know it, *Monsieur le Sénateur*?

Politics are not made with sentiments, maybe. But to snap one's finger at them, to base peace (falsely) on forgetfulness and – worse – on rewarding the most horrible crimes history has ever known: even a poor goatherd could see where that would end.

AGAINST AN INJUSTICE

Letter to General de Gaulle

11 February 1955

Mon Général,

I had put off reading *The Call to Honour* from week to week, for it is not one of those books one resigns oneself to reading in odd moments, glancing hastily over the pages – and I have not till now had the time to read it attentively.

Now, however, I am deep in it, and overwhelmed with memories, as I might have expected.

And yet why, when I reached page 231[1] should I have to find once more, and coming from your pen, the usual calumnies against the Communists? There are enough things with which to reproach them, without adding accusations which are historically untrue. For, *mon général*, I should be lying by omission if I did not bear witness on their behalf. The first letter I received, in August 1940, calling me to Resistance, was signed by the Communist Jean-Richard Bloch. The first meeting at which I was present in October, at the home of the poet Arcos, took place at the initiative of the same person, in the company of the Communist Frédéric-Joliot, the Communist Wallon, the Communist Maublanc, and the Communist Francis Jourdain, and at it letters from Eluard and Aragon, both of them in the unoccupied zone, were read to us. The first clandestine review, *La Pensée Libre*, founded in December, was a Communist review – and it was upon its ashes that I later founded the *Editions de Minuit*. The first clandestine organ of the *resistant* intellectuals was founded in April 1941 by the Communist Jacques Decour. It cost him his life. One of the very first resistants whom I saw something of, and who was later arrested almost under my eyes, and then tortured to death, was the Communist Holwegk. The first large scale 'affair' discovered by the Gestapo was that of the Musée de l'Homme, conducted by Communists. Like you, I said at the time to the Communist François de Lescure – then president of the Students' Association, and leader of the November 11th 'affair' – I said to him: 'All that separates us is wiped out, for the present. Perhaps when the war is over we shall fight each other again. But in the face of the enemy everything draws us together.'

When the war was over I found myself closer to them than I wished, and I have remained there to this day, precisely because of the injustices with which they have been showered, and of those calumnies to which your prestige has just brought a kind

[1] See pp. 270-1 of the English edition.

of historical justification. I cannot tell you how much it hurts me – when I consider today, with rage in my heart, what has been made of France without you, and without them. How far would she have gone, if you had managed in peace as in war to overcome your feelings towards them! If you had managed to use their love for the country – even if it is not of the same nature as yours – in the dangers of peace as in those of war! This divorce is, in my view, the supreme misfortune that has befallen France since that of the defeat. And this double estrangement, that which is imposed on them together with that which is imposed on yourself, constitutes in my view the main source of the mortal abasement into which we now see France being dragged.

Ought I to have written this to you? But reading *The Call to Honour*, and remembering such greatness and so many hopes, makes me aware, at the same time, of my sorrow and disappointment.

Reply to General de Gaulle

10 March 1956

Mon Général,

Your letter has moved me and surprised me. I thank you for not having forgotten me – nor lost confidence in me. (This is a feeling that has grown, in the last ten years, rather rare around me. . . .) I did not at first mean to recur to it – and to importune you. But it has occupied my mind during the whole of a journey from which I have just come back. And above all, I should like to tell you, in the first place, how sorry I am not to have managed to express better the warmth and emotion your memoirs have aroused in my mind – I thought it was so self-evident! It is precisely because it is obvious that our future historians will take practically everything concerning that period from your memoirs and probably from them alone, that I was saddened at finding in them a historical error which is in danger of being perpetuated. And so you have read in my reproach more than I had put there: I was far too pleased at the time for your attitude towards the Communists and the U.S.S.R. during the whole of the war, to have read absently or to have misunderstood the passages relating to it, when I found once more its living reflection in *The Call to Honour*. I have not forgotten, either, the way in which you did justice to them at the Liberation. I was speaking only of the short passage (a few lines) in which you take up again, against the French Communists, the current accusation of having abstained from Resistance until the entry into the war of the U.S.S.R. You object to my evidence that those were just a few individuals. But there, precisely, lies the injustice towards them: of what other party would you not say the same? What party was not at that time divided against itself? And what party in the first months of war suffered more than the Communist party from being broken into a thousand scattered pieces in search of one another in the night? And yet, what other 'party' brought out clandestinely a resistant review as early as 1940? The Radicals? The Socialists? The Moderates? What *réseau* issuing from a 'party' got to work before the Communist *réseaux*? Would you dream of reproaching the others for those long months spent in hesitation, in looking for one another, in getting organized? Would you find it reasonable to accuse them, on account of these delays, of obedience to Rome or to the White House rather than to France? Would you hold me suspect for not having written *The Silence of the Sea* till 1941, and published it only in 1942? To reproach the Communists with the same delays, seize on a coincidence (a very indistinct one, at that!) of dates as a stick to beat them with – is not this to turn a mere prejudice against them into a false certainty – in other words to commit a profound injustice?

There may, of course, *mon général*, exist Communists misguided enough to put the interests of the U.S.S.R. before those of France – just as there exist Rightists blind enough to put before those of France the interests of America, and even of Germany. If there are separatists, they are in all the camps. And as for me, *mon général*, I see far more of them in my own class than among the Communists. Where are the real 'running dogs' of today? But if you look back, where do you see those who have done the most harm to France during these terrible ten years? Were they those who kept striving for negotiation in

Indo-China, or those who refused them for sordid reasons until the collapse? Those who have so long been asking that France should render justice to the populations of Africa, or those who make their minds up to that reluctantly, too late as always, when the knife is at their throat? Those who continue desperately trying to retard German rearmament, or those who see to it that the A-bomb may soon find its place in the arsenals of the Reich? The Communists, *mon général*, have abused you – they abused me too when I expressed doubts about the working of justice under popular democracy, they are quick on the draw when offended (and others are quick on the draw against them, you must admit), but I can bear witness that they are, in their way, more punctiliously patriotic than a great many others. The misunderstanding between them and you is a terrible and disastrous one.

Ah, *mon général*, this is a very long letter, and you may find my insistence importunate, even out of place. But, you see, I cannot console myself. Who – what man with enough authority – could at this stage appear suddenly on the soil of Algeria and make himself heard by everyone – who, except you? But who would send you there? No one – if not the will of the people, if it could. And this will goes, at present, through the Communists. This is perhaps a lot of illusions, evidence of a somewhat delirious imagination. That may be. When you left for London, almost unknown, and alone, that also was slightly delirious. A delirium which saved France can probably not be repeated a second time.[1]

Forgive me, *mon général*, these too long and somewhat extravagant remarks. They will at least have relieved my heart.

Letter to Jules Isaac

1 November 1954

Thank you for your kind letter – in spite of the divergencies which it brings out between us, but are not these fruitful? Your

---

[1] This judgement, expressed in '55, may seem, five years later, both prophetic and erroneous. But de Gaulle chose to take power with extreme right-wing support. No wonder that, after more than two years, he has still not been able to restore peace in Algeria, since he will have to impose it against his own troops – i.e. by seeking support from the working-class.

views keep me on the alert, when perhaps I might be tempted to believe too much in what I have seen (in China, in the U.S.S.R.); and what I have seen and say may also, I hope, hold you back from believing the opposite too blindly and falling for lies told here. . . .

I must say, though, there is one point on which I am still sensitive: that of being misread. Not so much for my own sake: but as a sign of the part played by passion (even when it is very much held in check), of which even a man like you cannot rid yourself completely. I take up again, in fact, what you tell me about your leaving the C.N.E. (which had by no means passed unnoticed by me!).

You left because Martin-Chauffier, then president, did not force *Lettres Françaises* to make a correction.[1]

If you had read me properly you would have seen that you cannot accuse him of that. H—— left for the same reasons as you. But the C.N.E. page was a guest and had no rights. And that did, in fact, create a confusion: it suggested that what was said in the *Lettres Françaises* committed the C.N.E. also, and that what the C.N.E. said committed *Lettres Françaises*. Would the idea of asking the president of the C.N.E. for a correction in the *Lettres Françaises* have come into your head if the C.N.E. page had appeared, let us say, in *L'Observateur*? That it was a mistake for it to appear in the *Lettres Françaises* I was myself so convinced, that one of my first acts as president was to put a stop to that confusion and get the executive committee to agree to the suppression of the C.N.E. page in the *Lettres Françaises*. A painful sacrifice, because naturally no other periodical will have us.

On the other hand, you do not reproach Martin-Chauffier, as president, with what he really did. For the whole C.N.E. affair certainly did not at all centre on the question of whether there was or was not state anti-Semitism in the Communist countries (we will return to that). It centred on the following fact:

H—— had already protested in November. Neither the president of the C.N.E. nor Groussard nor anyone else had at that time done anything. Nobody at that time, except H——

---

[1] In respect of a rather scandalous article about the Jews and Zionism at the moment of the Slansky affair and that of the 'white-coated assassins'.

and you, resigned or even raised a voice. But when Vercors, three months later, became president in his turn, the same Martin-Chauffier, Groussard, etc. . . . immediately let fly. Why?

That is what needs thinking over, you see: what were their real aims in brandishing that sudden indignation, which ought to have made itself heard even louder three months earlier (before Gottwald had published in the *Rude Pravo* his article against all anti-Semitic tendencies)? What is really *intolerable* is that people shut their eyes to anti-Semitism when it suits them and brandish it as a matter of conscience when this becomes politically useful. To me the most odious thing of all is this cold duplicity.

For the rest, I can merely tell you that in my heart and conscience, what I have seen and heard in the U.S.S.R. makes me convinced that anti-Semitism only exists there as it exists everywhere else – and first of all in France. But that it is not a government policy. After all, you never hoped, surely, that any imaginable power (even the most just, even the most humane) could destroy anti-Semitic feelings in the hearts of *all* its subjects? Did you suppose that the Soviet bureaucracy was the monolith it is here claimed to be? It is going to be a long, very long, labour, as you well know. And there will be more than one relapse. But when writers like Simonov and Polevoï assure me that, *for them,* anti-Semitism is as unthinkable as cannibalism, I believe them. Just as over here I believe Domenach or Camus even though I know that in the nationalized industries there is certainly a *numerus clausus – de facto* if not *de jure*; and that even the lobbies of the Assembly swarm with intrigues against 'the Jew Mendès'. . . .

So that we ought not to be in disagreement, except on one point: the question of *how and with whom* to fight against lies, wherever they come from. Yes, on that point I can understand your not being with me. Twenty years of accumulated experience have made up my mind: I make no distinction between the lies but I do between the liars. One can lie in order to kill, or in self defence. I will never take sides with the first against the second, even if I refuse to endorse the latter's lies: I will do what I can to persuade them to defend themselves by better means, to show them that they are in danger of waking up one day to find themselves just like the others. But I should be horrified if the enemy profited by my doing so to make his own lies pass as truths.

And when I see that people are accusing the U.S.S.R. of 'becoming' anti-Semitic, the better to rearm against her the Germans who really built the ovens of Auschwitz, then I tremble with anger.

Letter to Jules Isaac

25 June 1956

I, too, at every turning point of my life, find once again our loyal and affectionate disputes! They force me to be more exact, to do some pruning, and to verify if I have really said what I thought and really thought what I have said. But I too 'cannot see why it should be necessary to reject freedom of thought'![1] I reject this dilemma, as you do: that is exactly what I mean! What I reject is, precisely, that people should try to impose this dilemma on me! As if the revolt of the masses, who want to be *able* in their turn to think, must inevitably deprive the 'free thinkers' of that freedom! That is the false dilemma which I denounce, and on this point I will never give way. And the revelations of the Twentieth Congress in Moscow, far from disturbing me, confirm me in my certainty. For if I was right, as opposed to the opportunists of Communism, when I refused to believe their statements about Tito and Rajk, I was also right as opposed to those who denied to Communism even the hope of a reparation. What a fine proof of the fact that thought is *never* stifled in a human society, as long as this society is not pursuing some diabolical dream like anti-human Nazism – not even after thirty years of silence and tyranny! The proof is there: if Hitler had won, can you imagine at his death his Nazi successors accusing him of having lied? Of having massacred the Jews? Was a single Maurras found ready to accuse Colonel Henry after his suicide and to rehabilitate Dreyfus? For twelve years I have never ceased to take as my refrain the fact that, in the U.S.S.R. and elsewhere, through fear or opportunism, the social revolution has been made to follow paths that were use-

[1] (In order to overturn the established order.)

lessly cruel and dishonest. But I have always refused to make this into a weapon against the revolution itself, or allowed it to be used as a weapon. This, no doubt, is why I am practically, apart from my books, reduced to silence: the *Lettres Françaises* are as closed to me as *Figaro* or *L'Express*. And I have just resigned from being president of the C.N.E. because the rôle of arbiter does not suit me any more, now there is no longer a danger of segregation arising in it between partisans of the East and of the West; and because I want to be able to say what I think is useful, even if this is embarrassing to one group or another. This is often tiring and depressing, but I can see no other rôle for a writer than to be critical, but loyal. And I have faith: in Man's will, despite his darkest errors, to build a *human* universe. This is why I do my feeble best to aid them, and if I succeed even a little, what more can I ask? My short story *A Political Lie*, from *Les Yeux et la Lumière*, is revolutionizing Warsaw, it appears. It will have taken eight years. Not long, really.

Thank you for your two reprints and for *Genèse*, in which I am engrossed at this moment.

AGAINST AN ACT OF BLINDNESS[1]

French Communists, my friends!

Some of the signatories of this appeal supported you for a long time, then fought against you because they did not accept your endorsement of trials that were too patently framed: others, on the contrary, though they too neither accepted these nor remained silent about them, still gave you, none the less, a difficult loyalty, knowing that for them it would mean a great loneliness, since it would cost them the greater part of their audience without having won for them yours; and others, lastly, came to you just when the first were leaving you, understanding that, after all, you represented the mass of the working people, without which no one is anything.

[1] This appeal, written at the end of November 1956, on the instigation of a prominent 'Democratic-Communist', was intended to be signed by several well-known names, and sent to the Central Committee, but to be kept private. It was circulating when the already grave unrest in Hungary broke out into insurrection and at once rendered this appeal obsolete.

All of them are agreed today, beyond those long-standing divergencies, to speak to you with a single voice. Knowing, as they do, that their voice expresses not only their personal anguish, but, through them, that of millions of non-Communist Frenchmen, who have voted for you and who today are wondering, doubting, moving away and losing both their hope and the trust they had placed in you. For the issue is no longer one of persons, nor of tactical disagreements, nor even of opposed moral ideas. It is no longer even a matter of reproaches for your past attitude – and the *mea culpa* statements of some of your people, who obstinately refused to listen when we were giving warning after warning, have inspired in us more embarrassment than reassurance. It is not a question of the past, but of the future. What is at issue is the future of France, it is to spare our country a series of disasters which, interspersed perhaps with a few ephemeral successes, would, in the long run, become heavier than those of '40, because they would end in France being alone, hated by a thousand million people and disavowed by her own friends. The issue is to stop this abominable downward slide, and there is only one way of doing so: the union of all the workers, Communist, Socialist and Christian, and also of that part of the lower and upper middle class which is known as 'enlightened' because it is in fact perhaps beginning to see daylight.

To make this union a reality, two conditions must be observed: that the French Communist Party itself should be united, but its apparent union is no longer more than a repainted façade. And that it should recover, among the others, a confidence it has long ago lost.

Those of us who, in spite of a very great temptation, consented none the less to remain silent during these last six months, kept this difficult silence in the hope it would help you to carry out in your turn, without damage, the revision which the Party in China managed to do in good time, which the Party in Poland did though rather late, and which the Party in Hungary tried to do much too late. You are not, of course, threatened with the same outbursts. But the divisions of which these are the expression will inevitably take place also within your ranks.

Everywhere the labouring masses have shown that they will not
in the long run accept a Socialism that sacrifices its moral bases
(you dislike this word 'moral' but it is stronger than you) to
tactical ends. More than bread and circuses, their great demand
is still bread and justice. It is not a handful of intellectuals here
and there who have set events in motion: they have only, and
you know it, reflected what is a profound revolt in their people.
In France this revolt is still sleeping, but it will awaken.
Certainly you can, by the silence of your Press, delay this
awakening, you will merely make it the more destructive to the
Party the more time you lose.

And how will you recover the confidence of our people, and
first of all of the Socialist workers, by acting as you are doing?
You thought it was enough to vote full powers to the leader of
their Party? By doing so you were abandoning all those,
Radicals, Socialists and Communists – who were trying to
oppose a mad policy. It was a vain compromise, because you
got nothing except further isolation. And what discussion do
you imagine the workers can begin among themselves with
a view to common action, when, on the gravest question, yours
have no answers but ignorance? The 'so-called' Krushchev
report, the Eighth Congress at Peking, Rajk, Poznan and the
Hungarian effervescence – of all these you have hidden as much
as you could, and those of your militants who are nevertheless
perturbed must read the *bourgeois* Press. But what then do you
hope to achieve? Where do you think this ostrich behaviour can
lead you in the long run? We beg of you, precisely because we
dread a break up of your Party as a catastrophe, pull yourselves
together! Show, by a few striking decisions, that you are no
longer afraid of the effect of truth on your own troops, that you
seek support from now on in their wisdom and not in their
ignorance, obedience or passivity, and that the French Communist Party also is capable of finding the right way, with
justice and frankness. Open *L'Humanité* to frank discussion, give
back to your friends freedom of speech in the *Lettres Françaises*,
under guarantee by a committee of writers who come from
the Resistance. If you delay, union will of course occur none the
less. But it will come too late, over the ruins of France, in the

teeth of the savage dictatorship of a Fascism that is on the watch for its revenge and is rejoicing every day over your hesitations.

AGAINST AN OBSTINACY[1]

In a few weeks' time it will be eight years since the victories of the Chinese People's Army sounded the awakening of China, and five years ago this evening, almost to the day, the Franco-Chinese Friendship Association was founded.

Have no fear, I am not going to impose on you a historical review. But it is of some use, none the less, for us to turn back and look at the past, to see if we have the right to think we have served some purpose.

When we formed our Association, we had two main objectives. The first was a very general one: to help China and France to get to know one another. The second was more particular: to help them to 'recognize' one another. China is five thousand years old. France much less (although she is one of the oldest nations of Europe). Up to last century, in spite of their age, our two countries knew each other hardly any better than if one of them had been on the moon. It was necessary for modern technique to shorten distances before the first real exchanges – I mean by this, mutual understanding – could at last take place, some sixty or eighty years ago. But up to the middle of this century, that is to say until the last few years, these exchanges, this knowledge and understanding, had hardly extended outside the circle of specialists. What did a man like me, for example, know of China when he set out, four years ago this autumn? Almost nothing. To realize that this evening fills me with astonishment. It seems to me now as if China had always been so familiar to me! And the most extraordinary thing is that it should have become likewise familiar to so many French people who have never gone to China. This double phenomenon of ignorance and familiarity, not to say fraternity, the one taking the other's place in so short a time after centuries of inert indifference, deserves examination. What are its causes?

[1] Opening speech for the fifth anniversary of the foundation of the Franco-Chinese Friendship Society (Pleyel., June 1957).

Well, I think our ignorance of China till lately came from the same egoistic feeling which keeps the normal man away from hospitals and prisons. If you go and visit Avignon, Rome or Amsterdam, unless you have the heart of St. Vincent de Paul, you don't go there to visit hospitals and prisons, although certainly the inmates of those establishments deserve more than anyone that you should take an interest in their fate. But you can do so little for them! This powerlessness keeps you at a distance, and if by chance you visit the Hospice of Beaune, you do so in spite of and not because of its patients; and if I sometimes felt regret at not being able to tour China, it was in spite of, and not because of, China's squalid slums. For the last hundred years China had been decaying and dying. The exotic appeal of poverty has always repelled me, I hate picturesque slums, and when, three years ago, I visited an appalling *medina* in which I did not succeed in meeting with a single healthy child, my one idea was to take the next boat home. As quickly as possible. That is like the story of Rothschild having the tramps turned away because the sight of them breaks his heart; but Rothschild could do something and I could not. So it was for China in the past. I could do nothing for five hundred million Chinese; and I did not feel the inhumane desire of the tourist to know that torn country, sucked dry to the marrow by the whole of imperialist Europe – the tourist who must arm himself with indifference if he is to enjoy his sightseeing.

That is what made a certain man who went there as a tourist for three weeks stay there for – it will soon be thirty years: he is still there. It gives me pleasure to mention that exemplary man here tonight. His name is Rewi Alley. He landed one day at Shanghai, I think, coming from New Zealand. A week later, horror at the condition of the Chinese had so overwhelmed him that he thought: 'There is no middle way: either I must escape by the first boat, or else stay with these wretched people and try to help them.' *I* escaped from that *medina*, but he stayed in China. With what hope? I wonder. Thirty years ago you had to be called Mao Tse-tung to dare believe that China's destiny was not hopeless.

It was not, and men like Rewi Alley have received their

reward: when they see their pitiable and oppressed China today rapidly becoming one of the foremost powers in the world, I wonder which is uppermost in their minds – happiness or pride? As for us, we gather fruit without having risked anything – either our suffering, or even our confidence. We experience, without having any right to them, this familiarity and brotherhood which have taken the place of our ignorance. The hospitals and prisons of Rome and Amsterdam have become parks and builders' yards filled with singing and laughter! So we visit them, or die to do so. And high time, too. It's not perhaps a thing to say on a day of celebration, and better late than never, but all the same it was high time in 1952 to think of Franco-Chinese friendship!

Now, this is self-criticism, unless I am much deceived. Yet we have an excuse: there are people who are much worse than we are. There are people who not only do not rejoice, but look back with regret to the time of the hospitals and prisons. Some of them from that detestable snobbery I have already mentioned – the taste for the exotic or picturesque in poverty. I will not name the intelligent man who boasted in my presence, only a few days ago, that the only things that interest him when he travels are the gambling-dens and prostitution – everything else bores him and he has no desire to go to China. Men like that are not the worst. The worst ones look back nostalgically to the old China because the new China defeats them, and because – horror of horrors! – it threatens Western supremacy and, with this, their well-being as a superior race. They would like to make of China a ghetto – a ghetto of six hundred million human beings – and since that is not possible they try to poke France into their ghetto, as the ostrich sticks its head into the sand. That is why, though late in the day and climbing on to the band wagon, our Association is not devoid of merit or utility. Our job is to prevent the ghetto closing in, not on China but upon France. Our job is to multiply our efforts to keep going all possible contacts between France and China. Have no fear, I have no intention, either, of distributing good marks for what we have done. Let it merely be remembered that, thanks to our existence, more French people have visited China in the last five years than in perhaps twenty-five years before; that these visits have since materialized – if I may put it like that – as books, pamphlets, articles, lectures and public discussions; that artistic events of the first order, like the revelation in Paris – and later in Rome and London – of the Peking Opera, are a direct result of our efforts; and that while in this way the French have got to know China, China also has got to know France, for we have received from China, apart from the Opera, the Circus, the shadow-play and puppet performances, a good many representatives of the arts and literature, of science and of industry – and I am not a little proud of the fact that the municipality of my own village was the first in the history of France to receive with great ceremony, a week before Paris, a Chinese cultural delegation. But above all, we have almost without cease done all in our power to make official France stop at last its absurd sulking and give the People's Republic of China political recognition.

I say 'official France' because France *tout court* has given this recognition a long time ago. And even various chunks of official France have already begun: in more or less all fields – business, industry, cinema, the arts – bits and pieces of camouflaged recognition, of a recognition that is unwilling to give its name, are constantly going forward. Our ex-ministers go to Peking to indulge, each for himself, in his own private little recognition – and reconnaissance. All this makes up an already quite considerable pile of bits and pieces of recognition, which, when the day comes, will reduce the Recognition, with a capital R – official Recognition – to a mere exchange of ambassadors: all the rest will already have been functioning for a long time (and for this we can take some credit). I wonder if history has ever known a more absurd situation. But let us not relax our efforts. We owe them to the two Chinas – the unhappy China of the past whom we never managed to aid, and the China of today whose vigour, wisdom, nobility and profound humanity excite our admiration and fraternal affection. We owe them above all to France, because our country has as much, indeed more, to gain in the future from China's friendship than China has from that of France.

The Southerner and the Negroes[1]

We must have the courage to look at things as they are! It is
unworthy of the men of a great country to be content with mere
words. I am not claiming to condemn in advance what is
going to happen, I am merely protesting against the good
conscience which people in France are getting ready to have
about it.

I address this to all our comrades of the Resistance, at least
to all those who have not gone racialist, in order to tell them
this:

If the Germans had won the war;

If they had made a third of France into a German province
and two or three millions of Germans had settled themselves
there;

Even if they had built bridges, harbours, dams and factories
– for them, not for the French: gradually driving the poor
peasants out from their land in order to appropriate it, and
turning a resigned population into a wretched troupe of starving
unemployed;

And if, after a hundred years of such an occupation, another
St. Joan of Lorraine had awakened the national feeling of these
too long crushed Frenchmen; and everywhere, at last, guerilla
warfare had broken out and *maquis* had been constituted;

And even if inexcusable and revolting atrocities had then
been committed against Germans who were more or less pacific:
German farmers, German teachers, German artisans and
engineers, who sincerely thought of themselves, after all that
time, as belonging to a country in which they had been born:
and even against some of the French who collaborated with the
occupiers;

Would you condemn the companions of the young woman
from Lorraine? Would you say that a hundred years are enough

[1] This article was offered in March 1956 to *L'Express*, which refused it because,
according to its editor, it never publishes any personal statement. And to *Libéra-
tion*, which abstained from publishing it for fear of being seized – which was in
fact probable. For this latter reason the author has thought it necessary himself to
censor his own text; the reader will therefore not be surprised to find the whole of
the end about Algeria blanked out.

for a country or a province no longer to exist, and for its population, if it revolts, to place itself outside the pale of humanity?

I am not saying that Germany ought not to intervene, nor saying she would not be obliged to protect her three millions of Germans; and while I am sure that, by executing as assassins all members of the *maquis* taken prisoner, she would merely precipitate a rising and massacres, I am not saying that Germany, in attempting to crush by military means this re-awakening of a French province, would be carrying out an illogical policy from the German point of view. The Southerner, William Faulkner, has just declared that justice is on the side of the negroes. That the Southerners are completely in the wrong; but that he is a Southerner and that, if one day it came to shooting, he would side with the Southerners against the negroes. At least he is not claiming that, by doing so, he would be defending justice and civilization; he knows, and admits frankly, on the contrary, that he would be committing, along with his people, an execrable action. He could not do otherwise, that is all. I should like us to have the same honesty as he has, before we commit ourselves to an action that will involve France, if she decides on it, in a long nightmare.............................

....

.... *(Censored by the author)* ....

....

That is all I have to say.

Good Pays for Evil [1]

I met the author of the following letter three years ago, when I went to Algeria for the first time. I went there to give some lectures. I had been asked not to talk politics. This although at that moment nothing seemed likely to happen over there, at least for a long time. On the contrary, coming from Tunisia where I had found a tense but healthy and lively atmosphere (it was six months before M. Mendès-France's flying visit), the Algerian population had seemed to me horribly resigned. I came from China. The contrast was unbearable. I could not

[1] Introduction to an Algerian letter for the Italian review, *Il Ponte.*

imagine such resignation to such poverty and such debasement.
All I could think of was to get away, to escape from that
monstrous spectacle, that sterile hopelessness. When the rising
began (and it was possible to hope that it would lead, as in
Tunisia, to rapid negotiations), I am willing to admit I felt
a kind of profound relief – so not all human dignity was
annihilated in those wretched rags! The insurgents were
bearing witness on behalf of Man and his indestructible
aspiration towards self-respect.

Later I was sometimes profoundly pained, even revolted, by
the excesses of terrorism. No cause has the right to kill innocent
people. But whose fault was it? What else can be expected, when
a whole people has lived in filth at the foot of luxurious dwellings built upon its distress and degradation? But the repression
with which the 'haves' strike down these 'have-nots' at the foot
of these same dwellings has a quality that is utterly loathsome.
Because it too kills innocent people, but they are wretchedly
poor innocents. That is revolting twice over.

During that visit I had met many people. Few of them
seemed to be aware of the reality; nobody then, even the well
informed, seemed to foresee that that volcano was sleeping with
only one eye closed and was on the point of eruption. A good
many people sighed, finding the situation frightful but hopeless.
A few compounded with it, perhaps rejoiced in it. All this was
in the highest degree atrocious.

One does not get out of a cruel situation without passing
through another cruel situation. How will the adventure end?
Three years ago all could have been saved easily. If France
loses Algeria, as she has lost Indo-China, she will lose much
more than Algeria. I foresee a new tragedy in France itself.
Meanwhile the tragedy is out there. What it amounts to – told
simply, without passion, in calm measured words – what it
amounts to for men of goodwill who cannot cut their hearts in
two, cannot resign themselves either to a savage victory against
a people which is finding once more its reasons for going on
living, or to a humiliating defeat for France, compromised and
dishonoured by her most impure elements, what the Algerian
tragedy amounts to for those men will be found in this letter.

It is not signed: that is because, over there, clandestinity is now the daily bread of free men as it was in France during the Resistance, even for those who did not take part in it armed, and as it will be again, in no distant future, if events follow their fatal course. Colonialism was not an undivided crime: there was a large part of nobility, even of human brotherhood, mingled with its basic iniquity and perversity. As always, the good pays for the evil. The France we love will pay for the Frenchmen we hate.

Letter to the President of the Republic

26 March 1957

The growing amount of information piercing through the official silence about the tortures in Algeria and the suicide – if it is one – of Maître Ali Boumendjel, which will remind all resistants of the suicide of Pierre Brossolette, fill us with shame and indignation.

A gesture like that of Professor Capitant must not remain isolated, protest becomes a civic duty. For my part, I have decided to return to you my insignia of the Legion of Honour into which I was asked to enter after the Liberation, at a time when it was indeed an honour of the kind one does not refuse.

Today I find it impossible to remain in it, when my country is covering itself not with honour but with odium.

.   .   .   .   .

With this letter to the Head of the State I close this political *dossier*. Not that I find it a good ending: but because, on the contrary, it seems a bad one. Indeed I have not the impression that this gesture of solidarity was keenly appreciated. Only one comment reached me, and that came from the anonymous contributor to a satirical paper which, on the whole, I rather like:

'. . . Nobody, clearly, will go so far as to think that M. Vercors, that great man of letters, is really only a rather sinister little man who never misses an opportunity of attracting, by some "public gesture" at least once a fortnight, a topical attention which persists in looking elsewhere. . . .

'... But let us not be unjust. Sometimes M. Vercors remains discreet. For instance, when the Russians pacified Budapest, the shame, indignation and fury which surely filled M. Vercors did not do so to the extent of overflowing.

'It is true that in that fortnight, having no Stalin Prize to return, M. Vercors had no future among the news items. ...'

Surely, people will say, you are not going to take the *Canard Enchainé* tragically? Excuse me. I often laugh heartily as I read the *Canard* – it expresses too widespread (and excellent) a section of public opinion on men and things for me to shrug my shoulders as soon as I am a target. ... And as for that diatribe, of course I take it with good humour – only, when an actor decides to play in a tragedy in which men are dying and being tortured, I am sorry, but he has not the right to get booed: he damages the play and his fellow actors in it.

Caesar's wife must be above suspicion, and so must the sincerity of the men who are fighting for justice. I cannot disregard this sign, whatever it may be. Besides, it is not the first, and I am indeed sorry, but clearly Vercors-who-wrote-the-sublime-book no longer enjoys the esteem or authority which still, not so long ago, gave his word, the weight to move, at least to some extent, people's wills and consciences. That is all over. The vase is cracked, I cannot help it. One must not be obstinate. For others the front place on the shelf, which I did not occupy for my pleasure. For me the silence of withdrawal, in which to grind – if I can – good grain into good flour.

.   .   .   .   .

Yet before I go I must carry out a duty which, though painful from a national – and human – point of view, is now demanded by simple equity.

It seemed to me, till now, that in face of the atrocious crimes of Hitler, of his S.S. and his Gestapo, no people other than his own was capable of so general and so deep a silence of complicity.

Today I have to recognize that, when I felt and professed these feelings, I was being unjust: since there are men of my own people who show themselves disposed to an equal cruelty; and since, in face of this cruelty, the French people shows itself at present disposed to an equal indifference.

Though less widespread so far, the same savagery is being repeated. The inhuman cries from the Villa Susini are already rivalling in reputation those which, in the rue des Saussaies[1] or from the cellars of the rue Lauriston,[1] obliged the neighbours to block their ears. I will not say whom those 'green berets', at whose approach men tremble at dawn, resemble, since already any non-clandestine writer is condemned to prudence – or to prosecution. Nor to what sort of 'Socialism', of sinister memory, the Socialism of certain ministers is now distorted – a Fascist writer can without danger congratulate them on it openly in *Rivarol*, but already resistant writers can no longer express alarm at it with impunity.

The men who still have the power to make themselves heard should take advantage of it: they are doomed, if the abominable business goes on, either to silence or to prison or exile. The worst thing is this: the people are silent. Even Germany, before the fall of the republic, did not experience such a silence. There were riots, often bloody ones, up to the last day. It is permissible to ask oneself if the French working class is not going to submit without a fight.

Should one then throw the helve after the hatchet? I am determined to answer firmly 'No'. And here, to conclude this long *dossier*, is a final song:

Ballad of The Wide Awake

Goats will scratch till they spoil their bed,
Pitcher to well too often wend,
Iron be heated till it's red,
Banged and bent till it crack and rend.
A minister has the use we lend,
Grows so remote he'll disappear,
And grows so bad he has no friend.
– Cry 'Noel' long enough, it's here.

[1] Gestapo headquarters in Paris.

He speaks till all he said's unsaid;
Embraces – no prize has he penned;
Promises – all his credit's fled;
Delays – the cause faints and is spent;
Hastes – it is broken beyond mend;
Busily – brings disaster near;
A tireless siege can no place fend.
– Cry 'Noel' long enough, it's here.

Princes, fools live to learn in the end,
Taken in till the lesson's clear,
Persisting till they apprehend.
– Cry 'Noel' long enough, it's here.
                                    Amen.

Ballad of Leave-taking

Here ends the Will and Testament
once and for all of poor Vercors.
Come to his grave for due lament
when the horn sounds – and best you wore
green like gherkins, and grieved no more.
Martyr to letters he will die:
this on his last button he swore
when to this world he'd say good-bye.

And what he said, I think he meant,
since he drowns where he swam before,
in his own vase, once ornament;
so that, from here to Périgord,
rightly or wrongly, either or,
he – so he says and it's no lie –
found only discord, civil war,
when to this world he'd say good-bye.

Though (be it said with his consent)
he was not very dead: what's more
– all fire and fury far from spent –
he felt biting him from skin to core
a sleepless itch for the great chore

of scribbling till he really die
(or till his hand be too sore)
When to this world he'd say good-bye.

Princes, mark his final score:
After breathing his last (public) sigh,
he took his pen, filled reams galore,
When to this world he'd say good-bye.
                    Amen.